Word 2007: Basic
Student Manual

Word 2007: Basic

Series Product Managers:	Charles G. Blum and Adam A. Wilcox
Writer:	Chris Hale
Developmental Editor:	Leslie Garrison
Copyeditor:	Catherine Oliver
Keytester:	Bill Bateman
Series Designer:	Adam A. Wilcox

COPYRIGHT © 2007 Axzo Press

ALL RIGHTS RESERVED. No part of this work may be reproduced, transcribed, or used in any form or by any means—graphic, electronic, or mechanical, including photocopying, recording, taping, Web distribution, or information storage and retrieval systems—without the prior written permission of the publisher.

For more information go to www.axzopress.com.

Trademarks

ILT Series is a trademark of Axzo Press.

Microsoft is a trademark or registered trademark of Microsoft Corporation in the United States and/or other countries.

Some of the product names and company names used in this book have been used for identification purposes only and may be trademarks or registered trademarks of their respective manufacturers and sellers.

Disclaimers

We reserve the right to revise this publication and make changes from time to time in its content without notice.

Axzo Press is independent from Microsoft Corporation, and not affiliated with Microsoft in any manner. While this publication may be used in assisting individuals to prepare for a Microsoft Business Certification exam, Microsoft, its dedicated program administrator, and Axzo Press do not warrant that use of this publication will ensure passing a Microsoft Business Certification exam.

Student Manual
ISBN-10: 1-4239-1831-2
ISBN-13: 978-1-4239-1831-8

Student Manual with data CD and CBT
ISBN-10: 1-4239-1833-9
ISBN-13: 978-1-4239-1833-2

Printed in the United States of America

1 2 3 4 5 6 7 8 9 10 GLOB 12 11

What is the Microsoft Business Certification Program?

The Microsoft Business Certification Program enables candidates to show that they have something exceptional to offer—proven expertise in Microsoft Office programs. The two certification tracks allow candidates to choose how they want to exhibit their skills, either through validating skills within a specific Microsoft product or taking their knowledge to the next level and combining Microsoft programs to show that they can apply multiple skill sets to complete more complex office tasks. Recognized by businesses and schools around the world, over 3 million certifications have been obtained in over 100 different countries. The Microsoft Business Certification Program is the only Microsoft-approved certification program of its kind.

What is the Microsoft Certified Application Specialist Certification?

The Microsoft Certified Application Specialist Certification exams focus on validating specific skill sets within each of the Microsoft® Office system programs. The candidate can choose which exam(s) they want to take according to which skills they want to validate. The available Application Specialist exams include:

- Using Microsoft® Windows Vista™
- Using Microsoft® Office Word 2007
- Using Microsoft® Office Excel® 2007
- Using Microsoft® Office PowerPoint® 2007
- Using Microsoft® Office Access 2007
- Using Microsoft® Office Outlook® 2007

What is the Microsoft Certified Application Professional Certification?

The Microsoft Certified Application Professional Certification exams focus on a candidate's ability to use the 2007 Microsoft® Office system to accomplish industry-agnostic functions, for example Budget Analysis and Forecasting, or Content Management and Collaboration. The available Application Professional exams currently include:

- Organizational Support
- Creating and Managing Presentations
- Content Management and Collaboration
- Budget Analysis and Forecasting

What do the Microsoft Business Certification Vendor of Approved Courseware logos represent?

Microsoft CERTIFIED Application Specialist | Approved Courseware

Microsoft CERTIFIED Application Professional | Approved Courseware

The logos validate that the courseware has been approved by the Microsoft® Business Certification Vendor program and that these courses cover objectives that will be included in the relevant exam. It also means that after utilizing this courseware, you may be prepared to pass the exams required to become a Microsoft Certified Application Specialist or Microsoft Certified Application Professional.

For more information

To learn more about the Microsoft Certified Application Specialist or Professional exams[1], visit www.microsoft.com/learning/msbc.

To learn about other Microsoft Certified Application Specialist approved courseware from Axzo Press, visit www.axzopress.com.

[1] The availability of Microsoft Certified Application exams varies by Microsoft Office program, program version, and language. Visit www.microsoft.com/learning for exam availability.

Microsoft, Windows Vista, Excel, PowerPoint, and Outlook are either registered trademarks or trademarks of Microsoft Corporation in the United States and/or other countries. The Microsoft Certified Application Specialist and Microsoft Certified Application Professional logos are used under license from Microsoft Corporation.

Contents

Introduction .... **iii**
    Topic A: About the manual... iv
    Topic B: Setting your expectations.. vii
    Topic C: Re-keying the course xi

Getting started **1-1**
    Topic A: The Word window 1-2
    Topic B: New documents 1-7
    Topic C: Word Help 1-18
    Unit summary: Getting started 1-20

Navigation and selection techniques **2-1**
    Topic A: Document navigation.. 2-2
    Topic B: Selection techniques 2-17
    Unit summary: Navigation and selection techniques 2-24

Editing text **3-1**
    Topic A: Working with text 3-2
    Topic B: Using the Undo and Redo commands.. 3-8
    Topic C: Cutting, copying, and pasting text 3-10
    Unit summary: Editing text 3-16

Formatting text **4-1**
    Topic A: Character formatting 4-2
    Topic B: Tab settings 4-14
    Topic C: Paragraph formatting 4-22
    Topic D: Paragraph spacing and indents... 4-30
    Topic E: Automatic formatting.. 4-36
    Unit summary: Formatting text 4-39

Tables **5-1**
    Topic A: Creating tables 5-2
    Topic B: Working with table content 5-7
    Topic C: Changing table structure 5-12
    Unit summary: Tables 5-19

Page layout **6-1**
    Topic A: Headers and footers 6-2
    Topic B: Margins.. 6-7
    Topic C: Page breaks 6-14
    Unit summary: Page layout 6-16

Proofing and printing documents **7-1**
    Topic A: Checking spelling and grammar 7-2
    Topic B: Using AutoCorrect... 7-12
    Topic C: Finding and replacing text 7-18
    Topic D: Printing documents 7-26
    Unit summary: Proofing and printing documents 7-30

Graphics   8-1
    Topic A: Adding graphics and clip art 8-2
    Topic B: Working with graphics 8-6
    Unit summary: Graphics 8-14

Course summary   S-1
    Topic A: Course summary S-2
    Topic B: Continued learning after class S-4

Quick reference   Q-1

Glossary   G-1

Index   I-1

Introduction

After reading this introduction, you will know how to:

A Use ILT Series training manuals in general.

B Use prerequisites, a target student description, course objectives, and a skills inventory to properly set your expectations for the course.

C Re-key this course after class.

Topic A: About the manual

ILT Series philosophy

ILT Series computer training manuals facilitate your learning by providing structured interaction with the software itself. While we provide text to explain difficult concepts, the hands-on activities are the focus of our courses. By paying close attention as your instructor leads you through these activities, you will learn the skills and concepts effectively.

We believe strongly in the instructor-led class. During class, focus on your instructor. Our manuals are designed and written to facilitate your interaction with your instructor, and not to call attention to manuals themselves.

We believe in the basic approach of setting expectations, delivering instruction, and providing summary and review afterwards. For this reason, lessons begin with objectives and end with summaries. We also provide overall course objectives and a course summary to provide both an introduction to and closure on the entire course.

Manual components

The manuals contain these major components:
- Table of contents
- Introduction
- Units
- Course summary
- Quick reference
- Glossary
- Index

Each element is described below.

Table of contents

The table of contents acts as a learning roadmap.

Introduction

The introduction contains information about our training philosophy and our manual components, features, and conventions. It contains target student, prerequisite, objective, and setup information for the specific course.

Units

Units are the largest structural component of the course content. A unit begins with a title page that lists objectives for each major subdivision, or topic, within the unit. Within each topic, conceptual and explanatory information alternates with hands-on activities. Units conclude with a summary comprising one paragraph for each topic, and an independent practice activity that gives you an opportunity to practice the skills you've learned.

The conceptual information takes the form of text paragraphs, exhibits, lists, and tables. The activities are structured in two columns, one telling you what to do, the other providing explanations, descriptions, and graphics.

Course summary

This section provides a text summary of the entire course. It is useful for providing closure at the end of the course. The course summary also indicates the next course in this series, if there is one, and lists additional resources you might find useful as you continue to learn about the software.

Quick reference

The quick reference is an at-a-glance job aid summarizing some of the more common features of the software.

Glossary

The glossary provides definitions for all of the key terms used in this course.

Index

The index at the end of this manual makes it easy for you to find information about a particular software component, feature, or concept.

Manual conventions

We've tried to keep the number of elements and the types of formatting to a minimum in the manuals. This aids in clarity and makes the manuals more classically elegant looking. But there are some conventions and icons you should know about.

Item	Description
Italic text	In conceptual text, indicates a new term or feature.
Bold text	In unit summaries, indicates a key term or concept. In an independent practice activity, indicates an explicit item that you select, choose, or type.
`Code font`	Indicates code or syntax.
`Longer strings of ▶ code will look ▶ like this.`	In the hands-on activities, any code that's too long to fit on a single line is divided into segments by one or more continuation characters (▶). This code should be entered as a continuous string of text.
Select **bold item**	In the left column of hands-on activities, bold sans-serif text indicates an explicit item that you select, choose, or type.
Keycaps like ⏎ ENTER	Indicate a key on the keyboard you must press.

Hands-on activities

The hands-on activities are the most important parts of our manuals. They are divided into two primary columns. The "Here's how" column gives short instructions to you about what to do. The "Here's why" column provides explanations, graphics, and clarifications. Here's a sample:

Do it!

A-1: Creating a commission formula

Here's how	Here's why
1 Open Sales	This is an oversimplified sales compensation worksheet. It shows sales totals, commissions, and incentives for five sales reps.
2 Observe the contents of cell F4	F4 = =E4*C_Rate The commission rate formulas use the name "C_Rate" instead of a value for the commission rate.

For these activities, we have provided a collection of data files designed to help you learn each skill in a real-world business context. As you work through the activities, you will modify and update these files. Of course, you might make a mistake and therefore want to re-key the activity starting from scratch. To make it easy to start over, you will rename each data file at the end of the first activity in which the file is modified. Our convention for renaming files is to add the word "My" to the beginning of the file name. In the above activity, for example, a file called "Sales" is being used for the first time. At the end of this activity, you would save the file as "My sales," thus leaving the "Sales" file unchanged. If you make a mistake, you can start over using the original "Sales" file.

In some activities, however, it might not be practical to rename the data file. If you want to retry one of these activities, ask your instructor for a fresh copy of the original data file.

Topic B: Setting your expectations

Properly setting your expectations is essential to your success. This topic will help you do that by providing:

- Prerequisites for this course
- A description of the target student
- A list of the objectives for the course
- A skills assessment for the course

Course prerequisites

Before taking this course, you should be familiar with personal computers and the use of a keyboard and a mouse. Furthermore, this course assumes that you've completed the *Windows XP: Basic* course or have equivalent experience.

Target student

The target student for this course is interested in learning how to use the basic features of Word 2007 to enter and edit text, browse documents, format text, use tables, insert headers and footers in a document, proof and print documents, and insert graphics.

Microsoft Certified Application Specialist certification

This course is designed to help you pass the Microsoft Certified Application Specialist exam for Word 2007. For comprehensive certification training, you should complete all of the following courses:

- *Word 2007: Basic*
- *Word 2007: Intermediate*
- *Word 2007: Advanced*

Course objectives

These overall course objectives will give you an idea about what to expect from the course. It is also possible that they will help you see that this course is not the right one for you. If you think you either lack the prerequisite knowledge or already know most of the subject matter to be covered, you should let your instructor know that you think you are misplaced in the class.

Note: In addition to the general objectives listed below, specific Microsoft Certified Application Specialist exam objectives are listed at the beginning of each topic (where applicable). To download a complete mapping of exam objectives to ILT Series content, go to: www.virtualrom.com/177E36353

After completing this course, you will know how to:

- Use the elements of the Word window, create and save documents, and access and use Help.

- Open a Word document; navigate by using the scrollbars, the keyboard, the Go To command, and the Select Browse Object button; switch document views; and select text by using the keyboard, mouse, and selection bar.

- Insert text, dates, times, symbols, and special characters; use the Undo and Redo commands; and cut, copy, and paste text.

- Change the appearance of text by applying character formatting; align text by setting tabs; format paragraphs by aligning them, adding borders, and applying bullets and numbering; change paragraph indents, line spacing, and paragraph spacing; and set AutoFormat options.

- Create tables; navigate, select elements, add text, and apply formatting in a table; and change the structure of tables.

- Add headers and footers to a document; set and change margins; and add and delete manual page breaks.

- Proof a document and use the thesaurus; use AutoCorrect to insert text automatically; find and replace text; and preview and print documents.

- Insert graphics and clip art; move graphics; modify graphics by cropping, rotating, resizing, and adjusting contrast in them; and wrap text around graphics.

Skills inventory

Use the following form to gauge your skill level entering the class. For each skill listed, rate your familiarity from 1 to 5, with 5 being the most familiar. *This is not a test*. Rather, it is intended to provide you with an idea of where you're starting from at the beginning of class. If you're wholly unfamiliar with all the skills, you might not be ready for the class. If you think you already understand all of the skills, you might need to move on to the next course in the series. In either case, you should let your instructor know as soon as possible.

Skill	1	2	3	4	5
Creating a new document					
Entering text and displaying nonprinting characters					
Saving a document by using the Save command					
Saving a document in a new folder					
Setting an AutoRecover time					
Renaming a folder					
Using Microsoft Office Word Help					
Opening a document					
Navigating and moving in a document					
Using the mouse, keyboard, and selection bar to select text					
Using AutoCorrect					
Inserting and deleting text					
Inserting the date and time					
Inserting a symbol					
Using the Undo and Redo commands					
Cutting, copying, and pasting text					
Finding and replacing text					
Applying character formatting					
Formatting multiple selections simultaneously					
Setting tab stops					
Formatting paragraphs					
Adding and editing bulleted and numbered lists					

Skill	1	2	3	4	5
Setting paragraph spacing and indents					
Creating a table and converting text to a table					
Navigating in a table and selecting table elements					
Formatting text in a table					
Adding and deleting rows and columns in a table					
Changing the width of a column in a table					
Aligning a table					
Creating and editing headers and footers					
Inserting page numbers					
Adjusting page margins and orientation					
Applying text flow options					
Adding and deleting manual page breaks					
Checking spelling and grammar in a document					
Finding synonyms and antonyms					
Printing a document					
Inserting graphics and clip art					
Controlling text flow around a graphic					
Modifying a graphic					

Topic C: Re-keying the course

If you have the proper hardware and software, you can re-key this course after class. This section explains what you'll need in order to do so, and how to do it.

Hardware requirements

Your personal computer should have:

- A keyboard and a mouse
- Pentium 500 MHz processor (or higher)
- 256 MB RAM (or higher)
- 4 GB of available hard drive space
- CD-ROM drive
- SVGA at 1024×768, or higher resolution monitor
- A physical printer is not required, but installing a printer driver is required for the activity titled "Using the Print dialog box" in the unit titled "Proofing and printing documents"

Software requirements

You will also need the following software:

- Windows XP, Windows Vista, or Windows Server 2003
- Microsoft Office 2007
- A printer driver (An actual printer is not required, but unless a driver is installed, students will not be able to complete the activity titled "Using the Print dialog box" in the unit titled "Proofing and printing documents.")

Network requirements

The following network components and connectivity are also required for rekeying this course:

- Internet access, for the following purposes:
    - Updating the Windows operating system and Microsoft Office 2007 at update.microsoft.com
    - Downloading the Student Data files (if necessary)

Setup instructions to re-key the course

Before you re-key the course, you will need to perform the following steps.

1 Open Internet Explorer and navigate to update.microsoft.com. Update the operating system with the latest critical updates and service packs.

2 If your operating system is Windows XP, then launch the Control Panel, open the Display Properties dialog box, and apply the following settings:
   - Theme — Windows XP
   - Screen resolution — 1024 by 768 pixels
   - Color quality — High (24 bit) or higher

   If you choose not to apply these display settings, your screens might not match the screen shots in this manual.

3 If Windows was already loaded on this PC, verify that Internet Explorer is the default Web browser. (If you installed Windows yourself, skip this step.)

   a Click Start and choose All Programs, Internet Explorer.
   b Choose Tools, Internet Options.
   c Check "Internet Explorer should check to see whether it is the default browser."
   d Click OK to close the Internet Options dialog box.
   e Close and re-open Internet Explorer.
   f If a prompt appears, asking you to make Internet Explorer your default browser, click Yes.
   g Close Internet Explorer.

4 If necessary, reset any Microsoft Word 2007 defaults that you have changed. If you do not wish to reset the defaults, you can still re-key the course, but some activities might not work exactly as documented. For example, if the Quick Access toolbar displays any custom buttons, then reset it. (Click the drop-down arrow on its right edge, choose Customize Quick Access Toolbar, click Reset toolbar, and click OK.)

5 To ensure that you can complete the activity titled "Setting indents" in the unit titled "Formatting text," set the following Word option:

   a Click the Office button and then click Word Options.
   b In the left pane, click Proofing.
   c Click AutoCorrect Options to open the AutoCorrect dialog box.
   d Activate the AutoFormat As You Type tab.
   e Under "Automatically as you type," verify that "Set left- and first-indent with tabs and backspaces" is checked.
   f Click OK to close the AutoCorrect dialog box.
   g Click OK to close the Word Options dialog box.
   h Close Word.

6 Create a folder named Student Data at the root of the hard drive. For a standard hard drive setup, this will be C:\Student Data.

7 Download the student data files for the course. (If you do not have an Internet connection, you can ask your instructor for a copy of the data files on a disk.)
   a Connect to www.courseilt.com/instructor_tools.html.
   b Click the link for Microsoft Word 2007 to display a page of course listings, and then click the link for Word 2007: Basic.
   c Click the link for downloading the student data files, and follow the instructions that appear on your screen.
8 Copy the data files to the Student Data folder.
9 To ensure that you won't get a security warning when you open files in Word, designate the student data folder as a Trusted Location:
   a Click the Office button and click Word Options to open the Word Options dialog box.
   b On the Trust Center page, click Trust Center Settings. The Trust Center dialog box opens.
   c Navigate to the Trusted Locations page.
   d Click Add new location. The Microsoft Office 2007 Trusted Location dialog box opens.
   e Click Browse and navigate to the student data folder.
   f Click OK to close the Browse dialog box.
   g Check "Subfolders of this location are also trusted."
   h Click OK to close the Microsoft Office 2007 Trusted Location dialog box.
   i Click OK to close the Trust Center dialog box.
   j Click OK to close the Word Options dialog box.
   k Close Word.

CertBlaster exam preparation software

If you plan to take the Microsoft Certified Application Specialist exam for Word 2007, we encourage you to use the CertBlaster pre- and post-assessment software that comes with this course. To download and install your free software:

1 Go to www.courseilt.com/certblaster.
2 Click the link for Word 2007.
3 Save the .EXE file to a folder on your hard drive. (Note: If you skip this step, the CertBlaster software will not install correctly.)
4 Click Start and choose Run.
5 Click Browse and then navigate to the folder that contains the .EXE file.
6 Select the .EXE file and click Open.
7 Click OK and follow the on-screen instructions. When prompted for the password, enter **c_601**.

Unit 1
Getting started

Unit time: 45 minutes

Complete this unit, and you'll know how to:

A Use the elements of the Word window.

B Create and save documents.

C Access and use Help.

Topic A: The Word window

Explanation

Word 2007 is a word processing application that is part of the Microsoft Office suite. A *word processor* is a program used to create, edit, format, and print documents, such as letters, reports, and Web pages. You can enter text, insert graphics and charts, print a document, and save a finished document as an electronic file for future use.

If you're accustomed to previous versions of Word, you might initially be disoriented by the new interface in Word 2007. However, Word 2007 is designed to give you easy access to every command and feature of Word, and the new features will make creating visually appealing word processing documents much easier.

Starting Word

To start Word, click the Start button and choose All Programs, Microsoft Office, Microsoft Office Word 2007. Every time you start Word, a new blank document appears in the application window, and the Home tab is active by default.

Components of the Word window

Word has several components you use to interact with the program. Exhibit 1-1 shows some of these components.

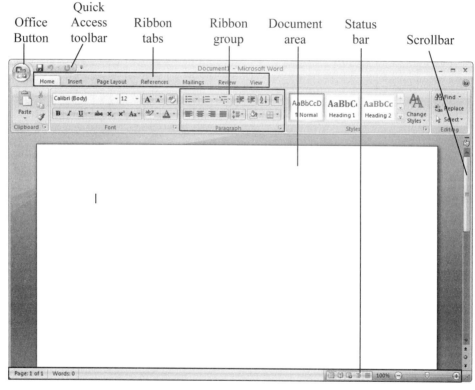

Exhibit 1-1: Components of the Word 2007 window

The following table describes the components of the Word window.

Item	Description
Office button	Displays a list of commonly used file commands, such as Open, Save As, and Print.
Quick Access toolbar	Contains buttons for frequently used commands. By default, Save, Undo, and Repeat/Redo are available. You can customize the toolbar to include additional commands.
Ribbon tabs	Contain Word's primary tools and commands, which are organized in logical groups and divided among the tabs. The main tabs are Home, Insert, Page Layout, References, Mailings, Review, and View.
Ribbon groups	Further organize related tools and commands. For example, tools and menus for changing font formats are arranged together in the Font group.
Title bar	Displays the name of the current document.
Document area	Displays the text and graphics that you type, edit, or insert. The flashing vertical line in the document area is called the *insertion point*, and it indicates where text will appear as you type.
Status bar	Contains the page number, word count, View commands, and document Zoom slider.
Scrollbars	Used to view parts of the document that don't currently fit in the window. You can scroll vertically and horizontally.

Galleries

In Word 2007, one way you can apply settings is to select an option from a gallery. *Galleries* provide icons or other graphics to show the results of commands or options, rather than providing simply a list of option names. For example, the Cover Page gallery (accessible from the Insert tab) displays small images of various built-in cover-page designs you can use.

In addition, some galleries and lists use *Live Preview*. When you move the pointer over options in a gallery or list that uses Live Preview, the format you point to is temporarily applied to the selected text or object. For example, pointing to a font in the Font list causes any selected text to appear temporarily in that font.

Do it!

A-1: Starting Word and exploring the program window

Here's how	Here's why
1 Click **Start** and choose **All Programs**, **Microsoft Office**, **Microsoft Office Word 2007**	To start Microsoft Word. By default, a new, blank document opens.
Maximize the window	(If necessary.) Click the Maximize button in the upper-right corner of the Word window.
2 Observe the title bar	Document1 - Microsoft Word The title bar displays the current document's name (Document1) and the program name (Microsoft Word).
3 Observe the items at the top of the Word window	The top of the window contains the Quick Access toolbar, Ribbon tabs, and Ribbon groups. These items are used to perform actions in Word.
4 Click [Office button]	(The Office button is in the upper-left corner of the Word window.) To display a menu of commonly used file-related commands, which you can use to open, save, and close documents. This menu also includes commands for finishing, sending, and printing documents.
Point to **Prepare**	To display options you can use to prepare a document for distribution.
Click [Office button] again	To close the menu.

5 Observe the Home tab		This tab contains the Clipboard, Font, Paragraph, Styles, and Editing groups, as shown in Exhibit 1-1.
6 Activate the Insert tab		(Click the tab.) To display its Ribbon groups.
In the Illustrations group, point as shown		
		A ScreenTip appears, describing the functionality of the Picture button.
7 Activate the Page Layout tab		
In the Themes group, click **Themes**	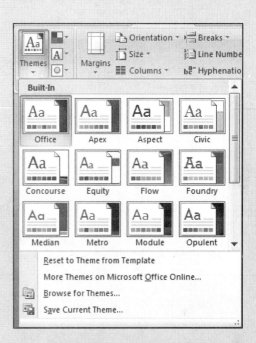	
		To display the Themes gallery. Galleries provide icons or other graphics that show the result of options or commands.
		Some galleries and lists also use Live Preview, which temporarily applies formats in the document as you move the mouse pointer over the options.
Click **Themes** again		To close the gallery.

8	In the Page Setup group, click as shown	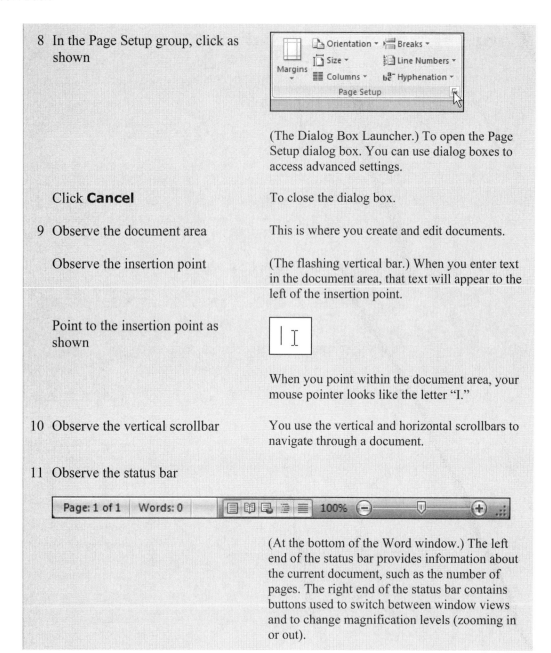
		(The Dialog Box Launcher.) To open the Page Setup dialog box. You can use dialog boxes to access advanced settings.
	Click **Cancel**	To close the dialog box.
9	Observe the document area	This is where you create and edit documents.
	Observe the insertion point	(The flashing vertical bar.) When you enter text in the document area, that text will appear to the left of the insertion point.
	Point to the insertion point as shown	
		When you point within the document area, your mouse pointer looks like the letter "I."
10	Observe the vertical scrollbar	You use the vertical and horizontal scrollbars to navigate through a document.
11	Observe the status bar	
		(At the bottom of the Word window.) The left end of the status bar provides information about the current document, such as the number of pages. The right end of the status bar contains buttons used to switch between window views and to change magnification levels (zooming in or out).

Topic B: New documents

This topic covers the following Microsoft Certified Application Specialist exam objectives for Word 2007.

#	Objective
1.1.1	**Work with templates** • Create documents from templates (This objective is also covered in *Word 2007: Intermediate*, in the unit titled "Templates and building blocks.")
1.4.1	**Customize Word options** • Set a default save location
6.1.1	**Save to appropriate formats** • Save as a .doc, .docx, .xps, .docm, or .dotx file (This objective is also covered in *Word 2007: Intermediate*, in the unit titled "Templates and building blocks" and in *Word 2007: Advanced*, in the unit titled "Forms.")

Creating documents

To create a document in Word 2007, click the Office button and choose New to open the New Document dialog box. Using this dialog box, you can create a blank document, create a blank template, or choose from a number of templates.

To create a blank document, open the New Document dialog box and click Create. (A blank document is created by default.)

Templates

Word 2007 includes several templates. In addition, many templates are available from Microsoft Office Online. If your computer is connected to the Internet, you can download these templates easily by selecting them in the New Document dialog box, as shown in Exhibit 1-2, and clicking Create.

Exhibit 1-2: Microsoft Office Online templates

Do it!

B-1: Creating a new document

Here's how	Here's why
1 Click ![icon] and choose **New**	To open the New Document dialog box. By default, the category "Blank and recent" is selected in the left pane.
2 Observe that Blank document is selected by default ![Blank document icon]	In the right pane.
Click **Create**	(In the lower-right corner of the dialog box.) To create a new, blank document.
3 Observe the title bar	The name of the current document is "Document2." The "2" is included because when you open Word, a new document ("Document1") is always opened by default.

Adding text

Explanation

When you open a blank document, you'll see the insertion point. As you type, the insertion point moves to the right, and the characters you type appear to the left. As you reach the end of a line of text, your text automatically wraps to the next line. This feature is called *word-wrap*. You can continue typing without pressing Enter to start a new line. When you press Enter, Word begins a new paragraph on the next line.

Nonprinting characters

Every time you press Enter, Spacebar, or Tab, Word inserts *hidden formatting symbols*, which represent actions on the keyboard. These characters, also called *nonprinting characters*, can appear on the screen, but not in the printed document.

Although they're hidden by default, you might find it helpful to see them when you're working with a document that contains a lot of formatting. You can turn these characters on or off by clicking the Show/Hide button in the Paragraph group on the Home tab. Exhibit 1-3 shows a document displaying nonprinting characters.

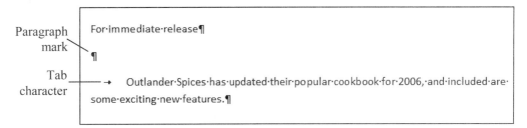

Exhibit 1-3: A document with nonprinting characters displayed

Do it!

B-2: Entering text and displaying nonprinting characters

Here's how	Here's why
1 Observe the document area	The insertion point is flashing in the upper-left corner. You'll enter some text.
2 Type **For immediate release**	The text appears to the left of the insertion point.
3 On the Home tab, in the Paragraph group, click ¶	(The Show/Hide button.) To show nonprinting characters. A paragraph mark appears at the end of the line you just typed.
4 Press ENTER twice	To insert two more paragraph marks.
5 Press TAB	For·immediate·release¶ ¶ → ¶ The arrow symbol is the tab character. You can use tabs to indent text.
6 Type **Outlander Spices has updated their popular cookbook for 2006, and included are some exciting new features.**	The text moves automatically to the next line when you reach the right margin.

Saving documents

Explanation

As you create documents in Word, it's important to save your work frequently. You save a document by using the Save and Save As commands.

The Save command

To save a document for the first time, you can use the Save command. You can also use the Save As command or use the Save button on the Quick Access toolbar.

To save a document for the first time by using the Save command, click the Office button and choose Save to open the Save As dialog box. Navigate to the desired location, and edit the File name box to give your document a name. Then click Save.

You can also use the Save command to save an existing document with its current name and in its current location. The Save command updates a file, writing to the disk any changes you've made. To quickly update a document, you can click the Save button on the Quick Access toolbar or press Ctrl+S.

Compatibility with older versions of Word

Word 2007 documents are saved with the extension .docx. Previous versions of Word used the .doc extension. Thus, in order for older versions of Word to be able to open and read documents created in Word 2007, you have to save them with the .doc extension. To do so, click the Office button and point to Save As to display other format options, as shown in Exhibit 1-4. Choose Word 97-2003 Format.

If you want to consistently save documents in the old .doc format, then you can change Word's settings so that this is the default. To do so:

1. Click the Office button and click Word Options.
2. In the left pane, click Save.
3. From the Save Word files as list, select Word 97-2003 Document (*.doc).
4. Click OK.

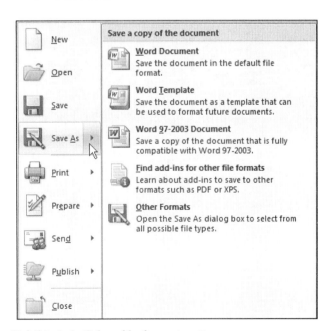

Exhibit 1-4: Other file format options

XML

Beginning with this version of Office, all Word documents use the Open XML format. This format makes it easier to use external data sources in Word documents, makes the content of Word documents easier to access in other applications, reduces file sizes, and improves data recovery. You still can save your Word 2007 documents in the previous format, though, to make them compatible with older versions of Word. In addition, updates to older versions of Word will enable those versions to use the new XML format. Finally, Microsoft will provide converter software to use with previous versions of Word.

Do it!

B-3: Saving a document by using the Save command

Here's how	Here's why
1 On the Quick Access toolbar, click 💾	(The Save button.) To open the Save As dialog box. This dialog box appears when you save a document for the first time. By default, this dialog box saves to the My Documents folder, and text in the File name box is selected. Word uses the first few words in the document to suggest the file name.
2 Observe the File name box	Word named the file "For immediate release" based on the document text.
Edit the File name box to read **My news release**	
3 Observe the Save as type box	Your document will be saved as a Word Document. This means it will have the extension .docx, which will not be compatible with earlier versions of Word.
4 Navigate to the current unit folder	Use the Save in list, located at the top of the dialog box.
5 Click **Save**	To save your document.
Observe the title bar	The title bar now displays "My news release" as the document name.

Creating folders

Explanation

When you save your documents, you store them in folders on your local hard drive or on a network. You can use the Save As dialog box to save the document in a new folder. You can also use the Save As dialog box to save a document with a new name.

To save a document in a new folder:

1. In the Save As dialog box, verify that the location where you want to create the new folder is selected in the Save in box.
2. Click the Create New Folder button to open the New Folder dialog box.
3. Enter the name of the new folder in the Name box.
4. Click OK to return to the Save As dialog box. The new folder is selected in the Save in box.
5. Enter the name for your file, and click Save to save the file in the new folder.

Converting a document to a different format

In the Save As dialog box, you can use the Save as type list to save a document in a different format, such as an XML document (.xml) or a Web page (.htm or .html). By doing so, you will give the document a file-name extension that's different from the extension for a Word 2007 document (.docx). Saving a document as a different type gives you the flexibility to send and share Word documents in a variety of formats that are suitable for different purposes and applications.

Do it!

B-4: Saving a document in a new folder

Here's how	Here's why
1 Click and choose **Save As**	To open the Save As dialog box. The Save in list displays the current unit folder.
2 Click	(The Create New Folder button is in the upper-right corner of the Save As dialog box.) The New Folder dialog box appears.
In the Name box, enter **My data**	To name the new folder.
Click **OK**	To close the dialog box. The Save in box displays "My data."
3 Edit the File name box to read **My press release**	
4 Click **Save**	The document's name has been updated in the title bar.

Using AutoRecover

Explanation

When you're working, you might forget to save regularly. This means that if Word closes unexpectedly, you might lose any work completed since the last time you saved. Word provides an automatic save feature that you can set to ensure that your documents are saved regularly. This feature, called AutoRecover, is found in the Save section of the Word Options dialog box. You can specify how often Word should automatically save a file.

To specify the number of minutes between automatic saves:

1. Click the Office button and click Word Options to open the Word Options dialog box.
2. In the left pane, click Save to display the save options, shown in Exhibit 1-5.
3. Check "Save AutoRecover information every."
4. Enter a new number in the box or use the arrow buttons to increase or decrease the minutes for the interval.
5. Click Modify and choose a new location for AutoRecover files.
6. Click OK.

Setting a default file location

By default, Word stores documents in the My Documents folder. Therefore, when you start Word and open a file, the contents of the My Documents folder are displayed by default, and when you save a file, it's placed in the My Documents folder unless you specify otherwise. However, you can change this setting.

To customize the default file location:

1. Click the Office button and click Word Options to open the Word Options dialog box.
2. In the left pane, click Save to display the save options, shown in Exhibit 1-5.
3. Click Browse, located to the right of the Default file location box, to open the Modify Location dialog box.
4. Navigate to the desired file location and click OK.
5. In the Word Options dialog box, click OK.

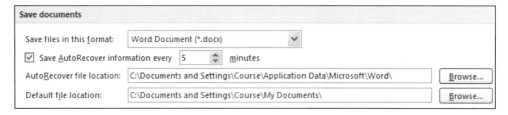

Exhibit 1-5: The save options in the Word Options dialog box

Do it!

B-5: Setting an AutoRecover interval

Here's how	Here's why
1 Click [icon]	
2 Click **Word Options**	To open the Word Options dialog box.
3 In the left pane, click **Save**	To display the settings for saving and AutoRecover.
4 Verify that "Save AutoRecover information every" is checked	This option is activated by default.
Set the time to **5** minutes	Edit the box to read 5.
5 Observe the default file location	Files will automatically be saved in and opened from this location. You can change this by clicking the Browse button on the right and navigating to the preferred file location.
6 Click **OK**	To close the Word Options dialog box. Your documents will now be saved automatically every 5 minutes.
7 Press ⏎ ENTER	To create a blank line.
Press TAB	To indent the paragraph you are about to type.
8 Type **In addition to recipes, the cookbook now includes sections on spice history and helpful descriptions of key spices.**	To add a second paragraph to the press release.
9 On the Quick Access toolbar, click [icon]	To save the changes in your document. Even though you've set AutoRecover options, you still need to save your documents.

Closing documents and closing Word

Explanation

When you've finished working on a document, it's a good idea to close it until you need it again. If you haven't saved your document before this point, Word prompts you to save before it closes the document.

You can close a document by clicking the Office button and choosing Close. After your documents are closed, you can close Word. To do this, click the Office Button and then click Exit Word.

Another method for closing documents, and for closing Word, is to click the Close button, located in the upper-right corner of the document window. If you have several documents open, then each time you click the Close button, the current document closes. If no documents are open, or if only one document is open, then clicking the Close button also closes Word.

Do it!

B-6: Closing a document and closing Word

Here's how	Here's why
1 Click [icon] and choose **Close**	To close your document.
	The default document, Document!, is still open, but you haven't modified it and thus don't need to save it.
2 Click [icon]	
3 Click **Exit Word**	(In the bottom-right corner of the menu.) To close Word.

Renaming folders

Explanation

You can change a folder name in Windows Explorer, however, you must first exit Word or you will get an error message. You can also rename a folder in the Save As or Open dialog boxes.

In Windows Explorer, navigate to the folder you intend to rename. To rename the folder, you must first select its current name by using any of these techniques:

- Click the folder to select it, wait a moment, and click the folder name to select it for editing.
- Right-click the folder and choose Rename.
- Select the folder and choose File, Rename.

When the folder name is selected for editing, type the new name and press Enter.

To change a folder's name in Word's Save As or Open dialog boxes, right-click the folder and choose Rename, or click the folder once to select it, and then click the name to select it for editing. When the folder name is selected for editing, type the new name and press Enter.

Do it!

B-7: Renaming a folder

Here's how	Here's why
1 Click **Start** and choose **All Programs**, **Accessories**, **Windows Explorer**	You can also right-click the Start button and choose Explore to start Windows Explorer.
Navigate to the Student Data folder	
Open the current unit folder	
2 Right-click **My data**	To display the shortcut menu for managing folders.
Choose **Rename**	The folder name is selected and ready for you to edit it.
3 Type **My press docs**	To rename the folder.
Press ← ENTER	The folder is still selected, but the name is no longer selected for editing.
4 Close Windows Explorer	Click the Close box in the upper-right corner of the window, or choose File, Close.

Topic C: Word Help

Explanation

You can use the Help system to get program information and instructions as you work. To access Help, click the Microsoft Office Word Help button in the upper-right corner of the document window. (If you're connected to the Internet, you can access online help information as well. To do so, ensure that "Connected to Office Online" appears in the bottom-right corner of the Word Help window.)

In the Word Help window, shown in Exhibit 1-6, type the word or term you want to search for and press Enter. The Help system works like a Web browser—each topic name is a hyperlink that, when clicked, displays information about that topic.

Exhibit 1-6: Microsoft Office Word Help

Do it!

C-1: Using Word Help

Here's how	Here's why
1 Start Word	Click Start and choose All Programs, Microsoft Office, Microsoft Office Word 2007.
2 In the upper-right corner of the document window, click	(The Microsoft Office Word Help button.) To open Word Help.
3 Observe the topics listed	(At the top of the window.) Browse the Help topics.
4 In the Search box, type **extensions**	
Click as shown	To display the Search options. Notice that All Word is checked, indicating that it's the default option.
Click **Search**	To search for Help topics containing the term "extensions."
5 In the Results list, click **Introduction to new file name extensions and Office XML Formats**	To display information about that topic.
6 Close Word Help	Click the Close button in the upper-right corner of the Word Help window.

Unit summary: Getting started

Topic A In this topic, you learned that Word 2007 is a word processor that you can use to type, edit, format, and print documents. You started Word 2007 and explored the **Word 2007 environment**. You examined components of the Word window, including the title bar, Quick Access toolbar, Ribbon tabs, document area, status bar, and scrollbars.

Topic B In this topic, you learned how to **create** and **save** documents. You saved a document by using the Save command. You used the Save As command to save a document in a different folder and with a new file name. You also **renamed** a folder. Then you added text to a document and examined the nonprinting characters.

Topic C In this topic, you used **Word Help** to search for information on a specific topic.

Independent practice activity

In this activity, you'll create a document and enter some text. Then you'll save the document in the current unit folder and in a new folder that you'll create. Finally, you'll close the document, close Word, and rename a folder.

1. Create a new document.
2. Type **Get materials together for press kit**.
3. Save the document as **My to do list** in the current unit folder.
4. Save another copy of the document in a new folder called **My practice folder**, within the current unit folder.
5. Close the document.
6. Close Word.
7. Rename My practice folder as **My Word practice**. Close Windows Explorer.

Review questions

1 How are the Save As and Save commands different from each other?

2 What are nonprinting characters?

3 How can you display nonprinting characters?

4 Is it possible to create new folders from within Word? If so, how?

5 What feature can you use to automatically save documents and avoid data loss?

6 What is the procedure for renaming folders?

7 How can you access online help for questions with Word?

Unit 2
Navigation and selection techniques

Unit time: 45 minutes

Complete this unit, and you'll know how to:

A Open a Word document; navigate by using the scrollbars, the keyboard, the Go To command, and the Select Browse Object button; zoom in and out on a document; and switch views.

B Select text by using the keyboard and by using the mouse, both in the document area and in the selection bar.

Topic A: Document navigation

This topic covers the following Microsoft Certified Application Specialist exam objectives for Word 2007.

#	Objective
5.1.1	**Move a document quickly using the Find and Go To commands** (This objective is also covered in the unit titled "Proofing and printing documents.")
5.1.2	**Change window views** • Split screen • Change zoom options

Opening documents

Explanation

Opening a document means that you're viewing its contents in Word's document window. The original document remains in the folder where it was stored.

To open a document:

1 Click the Office button and choose Open.
2 Navigate to the drive and folder containing the file.
3 Select the file.
4 Click Open.

Opening recently used files

The list of recently used files, shown in Exhibit 2-1, provides a way to open any of the last nine files you've worked on. To open a file from this list, click the Office button and select the file's name.

In addition, you can "pin" any of the files in the recently used files list so that they'll always be displayed in this list. Otherwise, as you open new documents, items in the list will be progressively moved down and will eventually be moved off of the list. To pin a file to the recently used files list, click the pin icon displayed to the right of the file name.

Navigation and selection techniques 2–3

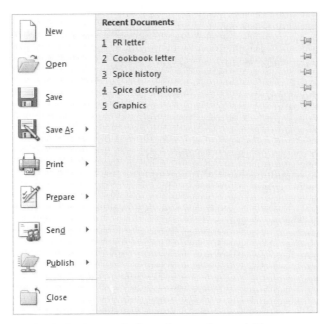

Exhibit 2-1: A sample list of recently used files

Do it!

A-1: Opening a document

Here's how	Here's why
1 Start Word	If necessary, click Start and choose All Programs, Microsoft Office, Microsoft Office Word 2007.
2 Click and choose **Open**	The Open dialog box appears. You can use it to navigate to different drives and folders.
3 Navigate to the current unit folder	
4 Select **Spice descriptions**	
5 Click **Open**	The Spice descriptions file appears in the document window. The name "Spice descriptions" appears in the title bar.

Explanation

Scrolling through documents

By default, Word displays about half of a standard 8.5"×11" page, so you'll often need to use navigation techniques to view all of the content in a document. You can use the horizontal and vertical scrollbars, the keys on your keyboard, or the Go To command.

Using the scrollbars

You use the horizontal and vertical scrollbars and your mouse to scroll through a document. *Scrollbars* are shaded bars displayed along the right side and the bottom of the document window. (Note that if the document fits horizontally in the document window, the horizontal scrollbar might not be displayed.) You use the horizontal scrollbar to scroll sideways. You use the vertical scrollbar to scroll the length of the document, page by page, screen by screen, or line by line. Exhibit 2-5 shows the components of the vertical scrollbar.

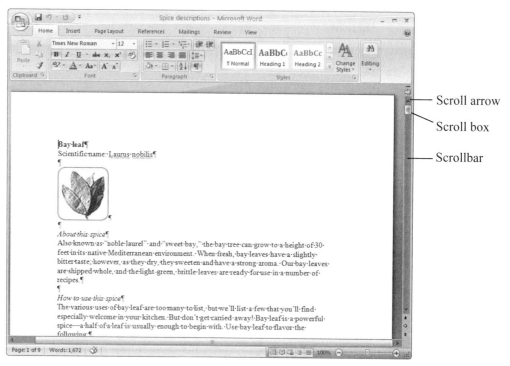

Exhibit 2-2: Components of the vertical scrollbar

The following table describes a number of scrolling techniques. Note that these techniques do not move the insertion point; they just change which part of the document is displayed.

Use these items...	To do this...	By...
Up and down scroll arrows	Move up or down one line at a time	Clicking the scroll arrows
Vertical scroll box	Move up or down, move to a specific page, or move to a heading on a page	Dragging the box along the vertical scrollbar
Shaded areas above and below the vertical scroll box	Move up or down one screen at a time	Clicking the shaded area above or below the vertical scroll box
Left and right scroll arrows	Move left or right one character at a time	Clicking the scroll arrows
Horizontal scroll box	Move left or right across a document	Dragging the box along the horizontal scrollbar
Shaded areas to the left and right of the horizontal scroll box	Move left or right one screen at a time	Clicking the shaded area to the left or right of the horizontal scroll box

Changing document magnification

By default, documents are displayed at 100% magnification. You can quickly change the magnification by using the Zoom slider, located on the status bar. You decrease the zoom level (reduce the magnification) by dragging the slider toward the minus sign. You can increase the zoom level (increase magnification) by dragging the slider toward the plus sign.

You can also change the zoom level by using the Zoom dialog box. To open it, activate the View tab and click the Zoom button in the Zoom group. (You can also click the zoom-level percentage in the status bar.) To quickly return to 100% magnification, you can click the 100% button, also located in the Zoom group on the View tab.

Do it!

A-2: Using scrollbars and Zoom options

Here's how	Here's why
1 Click ▼	(The down scroll arrow is located at the bottom of the vertical scrollbar.) To scroll down one line on the screen.
Click ▼ again	To scroll down another line.
2 Click the scrollbar below the vertical scroll box	To scroll down one screen in the document.
Click the scrollbar below the vertical scroll box again	To scroll down one more screen.
3 Point to the vertical scroll box, and press and hold the mouse button	A ScreenTip displaying the current page number appears.
Drag the scroll box to page 4	Point to the scroll box, press and hold the mouse button, and drag the box down until the ScreenTip displays "Page 4."
4 In the bottom-right corner of the document window, click as shown	To increase the magnification by 10%.
Increase the magnification to 150%	Click the plus sign four more times.
5 Examine the horizontal scrollbar	If a document is too wide to fit in the document window, you can use this scrollbar to move to the left and right in the document.
6 Reduce the magnification to 100%	Click the minus sign five times.
7 Return to the first page of the document	Drag the scroll box to the top of the vertical scrollbar.

Moving through documents

Explanation

You can use the keyboard or mouse to move through a document. When you *move* (as opposed to scroll) in a document, the insertion point moves. The following table shows ways to move in a document.

Use this key	To move...
Left Arrow	To the previous character
Right Arrow	To the next character
Ctrl+Left Arrow	One word to the left
Ctrl+Right Arrow	One word to the right
Up Arrow	Up one line
Down Arrow	Down one line
Ctrl+Up Arrow	Up one paragraph
Ctrl+Down Arrow	Down one paragraph
Home	To the beginning of a line
End	To the end of a line
Ctrl+Home	To the beginning of the document
Ctrl+End	To the end of the document
Page Down	Down one screen at a time
Page Up	Up one screen at a time
⤊	To the top of the previous page (This button is below the vertical scrollbar.)
⤋	To the top of the next page (This button is below the vertical scrollbar.)

Splitting a window

When you're moving through a long document, you might find it helpful to split the window into two sections, or panes, as shown in Exhibit 2-3. This enables you to see two different parts of a document at the same time. For example, you might want to check two sections to see if the formatting is consistent.

To split a window:

1 Activate the View tab.
2 In the Window group, click Split.
3 Drag the split bar to the desired location.
4 Click to split the window.

To remove the split, you can click Remove Split in the Window group, drag the split bar down to the status bar, or double-click the split bar.

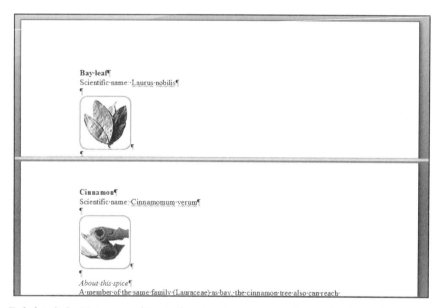

Exhibit 2-3: Using a split window to view two sections of a long document

Do it!

A-3: Moving in a document

Here's how	Here's why
1 Press PAGE DOWN	To move down one screen. The document window shows different content, and the insertion point has moved.
2 Click ▼	(The Next Page button is located below the vertical scrollbar.) To display the next page. The insertion point is at the top of the page. The page information in the status bar changes to reflect the new location of the insertion point.
3 Press CTRL + END	To move to the end of the document. The insertion point is at the end of the last word.

4	Click ▲	(The Previous Page button is located below the vertical scrollbar.) To move to the top of the previous page.
5	Press CTRL + HOME	To move to the beginning of the document. The insertion point is to the left of the word "Bay."
6	Activate the View tab	The View tab contains the Document Views, Show/Hide, Zoom, Window, and Macros groups.
	In the Window group, click **Split**	To activate the split bar. You can position it by using your mouse pointer.
	Click near the middle of the document	To split the document window into two panes.
	Point to the indicated area	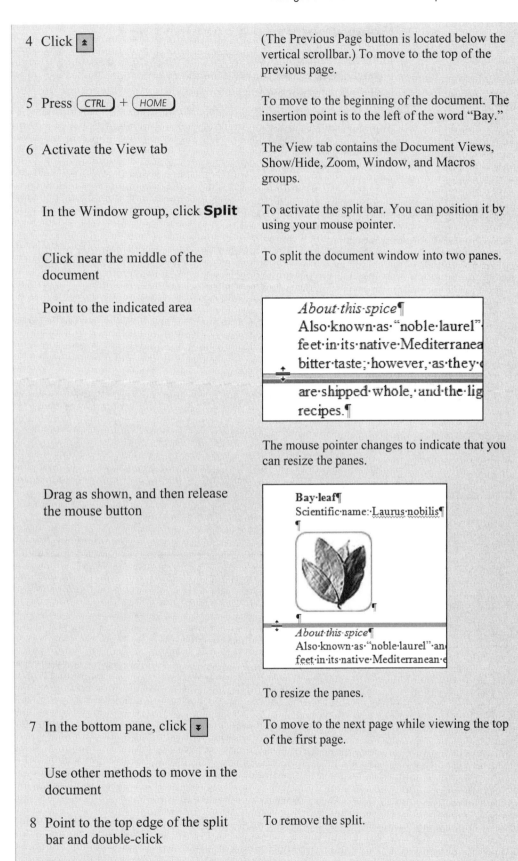 The mouse pointer changes to indicate that you can resize the panes.
	Drag as shown, and then release the mouse button	To resize the panes.
7	In the bottom pane, click ▼	To move to the next page while viewing the top of the first page.
	Use other methods to move in the document	
8	Point to the top edge of the split bar and double-click	To remove the split.
9	Return to page 1	(If necessary.) Press Ctrl+Home.

Going directly to a specific page

In a long document, it can be time-consuming to move to a specific location by scrolling through the document or pressing the Page Up and Page Down keys. If you know the page or line number you want to go to, you can use the Go To command to move quickly to that specific page, line, or other part of the document. The insertion point also moves when you use the Go To command, so you'll find it useful when you're editing a multi-page document.

Following are some ways you can quickly access the Go To tab of the Find and Replace dialog box, shown in Exhibit 2-4:

- Press F5.
- Press Ctrl+G.
- Click the "Page number in document" section at the left end of the status bar.

To use the Go To command to move to a specific page:

1. Open the Go To dialog box.
2. In the Enter page number box, type the number of the page to which you want to move.
3. Click Go To.

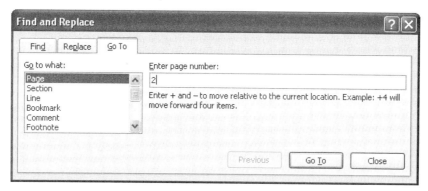

Exhibit 2-4: The Go To tab in the Find and Replace dialog box

Do it!

A-4: Using the Go To command to move to a specific page

Here's how	Here's why
1 At the left end of the status bar, click as shown	*Page: 1 of*
	To open the Find and Replace dialog box. The Go To tab is active.
2 Scroll through the Go to what list	Go to what: Page Section Line Bookmark Comment Footnote
	You'll see a list of options for where you can move in the document.
In the Go to what list, verify that Page is selected	
3 In the Enter page number box, enter **2**	As shown in Exhibit 2-4.
Click **Go To**	To move to page 2 of the document.
4 Click **Close**	To close the Find and Replace dialog box. The insertion point is flashing at the top of page 2.

Browsing by object type

Explanation

You can also move through a document by using the Select Browse Object button, which is located between the Previous Page and Next Page buttons, below the vertical scrollbar. The term *object* refers to document elements such as pages, sections, comments, tables, or graphics.

Clicking the Select Browse Object button displays a menu, from which you can choose an element of the document to browse. For example, if you choose Browse by Graphic, you'll go to the first graphic below the insertion point. You can then click the Previous Graphic and Next Graphic buttons to navigate from graphic to graphic. (These are the same as the Previous Page and Next Page buttons.) In addition, you can access the Go To command by using the Select Browse Object button.

Do it!

A-5: Using the Select Browse Object button

Here's how	Here's why
1 Verify that the insertion point is at the beginning of page 2	Page 2 contains the Cinnamon description.
2 Click	(The Select Browse Object button is between the Next Page and Previous Page buttons, below the vertical scrollbar.) The Select Browse Object menu is displayed in the lower-right corner of the screen.
Point to the buttons on the menu	The name of each button appears at the top of the Select Browse Object menu.
Select the indicated option	
	To browse by graphics. You've moved to the graphic on page 2.
3 Point to	The ScreenTip has changed to Next Graphic.
Click	To move to the next graphic, on page 3.
Continue browsing the graphics in the document	The last page in the document doesn't contain a graphic, so the Next Graphic button will stop at page 8.
4 Return the insertion point to the beginning of the document	Use any of the techniques you've learned to move the insertion point along with the display in the document window.

Print Layout view

Explanation

Word provides various ways to view a document. Each view provides certain features that are useful for different types and lengths of documents or for different purposes. For example, Draft view fills the screen from left to right and uses dotted lines to indicate automatic page breaks. (If you've used previous versions of Word, note that Draft view replaces Normal view.)

Print Layout view, which is the default view, gives you a sense of how a document will look when printed. As you scroll through a document in this view, the whole page is shown, including all four edges. This can create a large amount of white space if a portion of a page is blank.

In Print Layout view, you can hide this extra space. To do so, move the mouse pointer to the bottom or top edge of any page. When the mouse pointer becomes a tool to hide white space, double-click. Solid black lines now separate the document pages. To show the white space again, point to the solid black line and double-click.

Do it!

A-6: Using Print Layout view

Here's how	Here's why
1 Verify that the View tab is active	
Observe the Document Views group	The default view, Print Layout, is selected. This view shows you what your document will look like when it's printed.
2 Scroll through the document	For each page, you can see the four edges as well as white space near the top and bottom. This space increases when pages contain small amounts of text. If the page is completely blank, it's still shown in Print Layout view.
3 Scroll to the bottom of any page	
Point to the bottom edge, as shown	*Double-click to hide white space*
	The pointer changes its shape.
Double-click the mouse	(Use the left mouse button.) The white space is hidden, and a solid black line separates the pages.
4 Scroll through the document	The white space at the top and bottom of each page has been hidden.
5 Point to any solid black line	(The line that indicates the separation between pages.) The pointer changes again to indicate that if you double-click, you can show white space.
Double-click the mouse	To show the white space between pages again.
6 Return the insertion point to the beginning of the document	

Full Screen Reading view

Explanation

If you're reading a multi-page document on your computer screen, continually scrolling from one page to the next can become tedious. Also, when you're reading, you're likely not to need all of Word's editing and formatting tools, which take up space in the document window. You can use the Full Screen Reading view to improve the readability of a document by hiding the Ribbon and automatically scaling text and graphics.

To switch to Full Screen Reading view, activate the View tab; then, in the Document Views group, click Full Screen Reading. (You can also click the corresponding icon in the status bar.) Full Screen Reading view is shown in Exhibit 2-5. In this view, the document pages are referred to as *screens*. If only one screen appears in the view, you can click View Options and choose Show Two Pages. When you're finished reading, click Close to exit Full Screen Reading view.

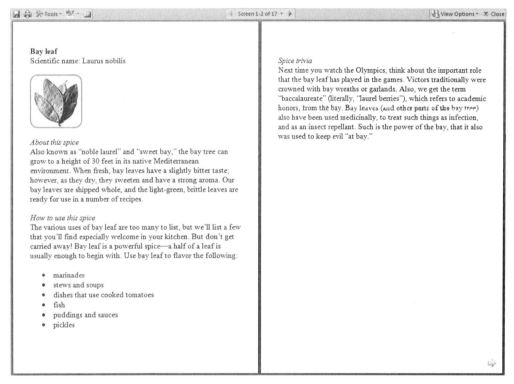

Exhibit 2-5: Full Screen Reading view

Do it!

A-7: Using Full Screen Reading view

Here's how	Here's why
1 On the View tab, in the Document Views group, click **Full Screen Reading**	To switch to Full Screen Reading view.
2 Click [→] twice	(Located in the bottom-right corner of the document window.) To turn to the page containing the information about cloves. In this view, the Cloves text runs over onto a second page. You'll check to see whether this will happen in the printed document.
3 In the top-right corner of the document window, click **View Options**	To display the View Options menu.
Choose **Show Printed Page**	To display the pages as they will appear when printed. The Cloves text will print on a single page.
4 Click **Close**	(In the top-right corner of the document window.) To exit Full Screen Reading view and return to Print Layout view.

Topic B: Selection techniques

Explanation

To manipulate a block of text or more than one section of a document at a time, you *select* the text by using the mouse or the keyboard. Selected text appears highlighted.

After you've selected the text, you can move it or copy it to another location within the document or to another document. You can delete the selected text by pressing Delete or Backspace or by typing new text to replace the selected text. By default, selected text is replaced by anything you type. So, while working with selected text, you need to be careful to avoid accidentally typing over it.

If you select some text, you can also deselect it. To deselect text, do either of the following:

- Click outside the selected text.
- Select other text.
- Press an arrow key.

Using the mouse in the document area

There are several ways you can use the mouse to select text. You can drag across the text you want to select, double-click a word to select it, or use a combination of the mouse and the Shift or Ctrl keys. By default, when you're dragging to select more than one word, Word automatically selects entire words. This means that if you begin dragging in the middle of a word and continue dragging to select additional text, the entire first word will be selected.

The following table describes basic techniques for using the mouse to select text.

To select...	Do this
A word	Point to the word and double-click.
A paragraph	Point anywhere in the paragraph and triple-click.
A group of words	Point to the beginning of the text you want to select, press and hold the mouse button, and drag the pointer across the text. Release the mouse button to finish selecting the text.
	Alternatively, place the insertion point at the beginning or end of the text, press and hold Shift, and click at the other end of the text.
A sentence	Point anywhere in the sentence, press and hold Ctrl, and click.
Text you want to add to a selection	To add to a selection, press and hold Shift, move the pointer to a new place beyond the current selection, and click.
	To add specific selections, press and hold Ctrl, and drag to select the specific text you want to add.
Text you want to remove from a selection	Press and hold Shift, move the pointer to a new place inside the current selection, and click.

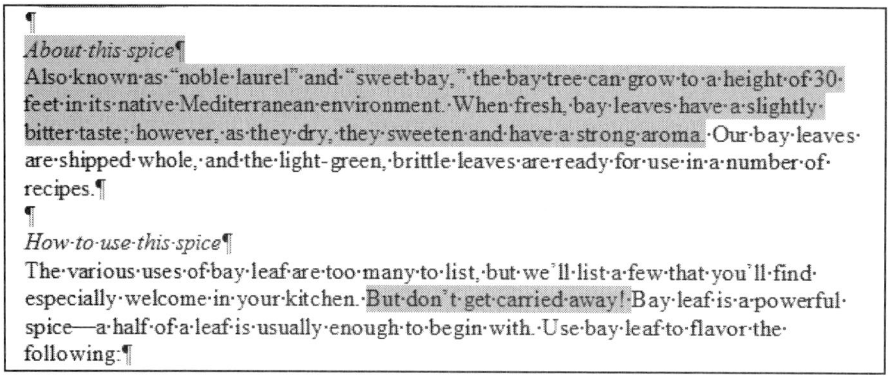

¶
About·this·spice¶
Also·known·as·"noble·laurel"·and·"sweet·bay,"·the·bay·tree·can·grow·to·a·height·of·30·feet·in·its·native·Mediterranean·environment.·When·fresh,·bay·leaves·have·a·slightly·bitter·taste;·however,·as·they·dry,·they·sweeten·and·have·a·strong·aroma.·Our·bay·leaves·are·shipped·whole,·and·the·light-green,·brittle·leaves·are·ready·for·use·in·a·number·of·recipes.¶
¶
How·to·use·this·spice¶
The·various·uses·of·bay·leaf·are·too·many·to·list,·but·we'll·list·a·few·that·you'll·find·especially·welcome·in·your·kitchen.·But·don't·get·carried·away!·Bay·leaf·is·a·powerful·spice—a·half·of·a·leaf·is·usually·enough·to·begin·with.·Use·bay·leaf·to·flavor·the·following:¶

Exhibit 2-6: Selected text in a document appears highlighted

Do it!

B-1: Using the mouse to select text

Here's how	Here's why
1 Return the insertion point to the beginning of the document	If necessary.
2 Double-click **Bay**	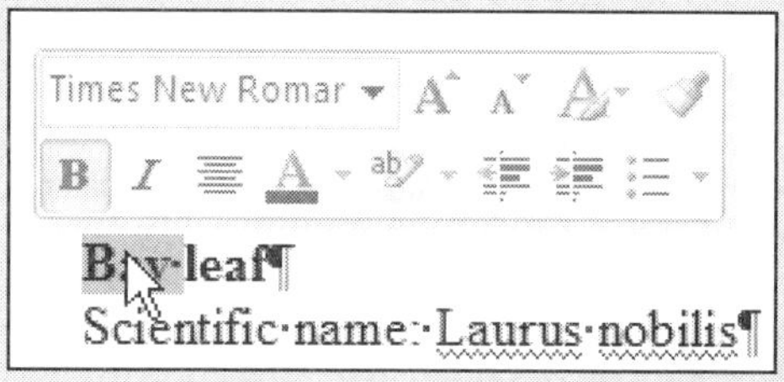 (At the top of the page.) To select the word. The Mini toolbar appears.
3 Place the insertion point as shown	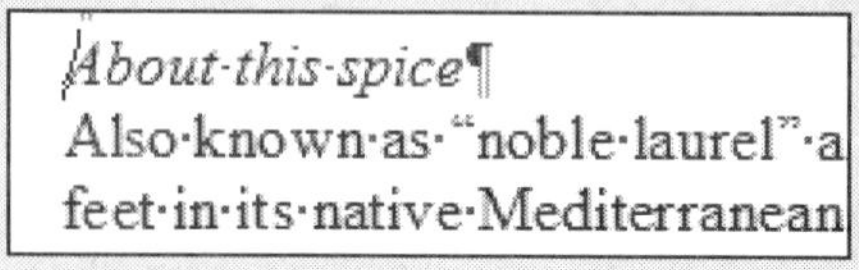 (At the beginning of the paragraph that follows the graphic.) When you click to place the insertion point, the word "Bay" is deselected.
Drag to the end of **spice**, as shown	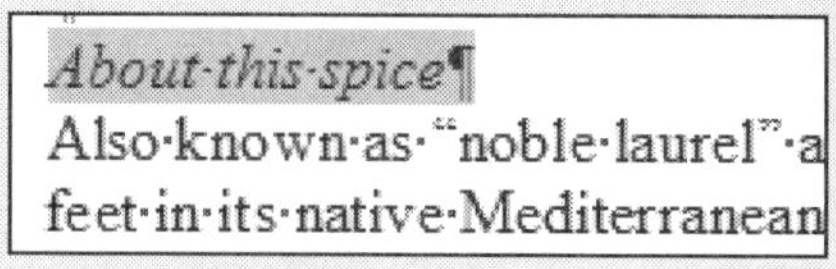 To select a range of text.

4	Press and hold CTRL	
	Drag to select **How to use this spice**	*About·this·spice¶* Also·known·as·"noble·la feet·in·its·native·Mediter bitter·taste;·however,·as are·shipped·whole,·and·t recipes.¶ ¶ *How·to·use·this·spice¶* The·various·uses·of·bay·
		To select additional text without deselecting the previous text.
	Release CTRL	
5	Click the page	To deselect the text.
6	Place the insertion point as shown	*How·to·use·this·spice¶* The·various·uses·of·ba especially·welcome·in· spice—a·half·of·a·leaf·
		(Just before the word "spice," three lines below "How to use this spice.") You'll select just the sentence containing this word.
	Press and hold CTRL	
	Click any word in the sentence	To select the sentence.
	Release CTRL	
7	Move to the top of page 1	
8	Place the insertion point anywhere at the beginning of the document	You'll select a range of text without dragging.
	Press and hold SHIFT	
	Click anywhere below the insertion point	To select a range of text.
	Click at another point below the text you've selected	(Be sure that you're pressing the Shift key.) To add to the selection.
	Release SHIFT	
9	Deselect the text	Click the page.

Using the keyboard

Explanation

You can use the arrow keys, the Home and End keys, and the Shift key to select text or other elements, such as graphics, in your documents.

The following table explains how to use the keyboard to select text.

Key	Action
Shift+Left Arrow	Selects the text to the left of the insertion point one character at a time.
Shift+Right Arrow	Selects the text to the right of the insertion point one character at a time.
Shift+Up Arrow	Selects text from the left of the insertion point to the same position in the previous line.
Shift+Down Arrow	Selects text from the right of the insertion point to the same position in the next line.
Shift+Home	Selects text from the left of the insertion point to the beginning of the current line.
Shift+End	Selects text from the right of the insertion point to the end of the current line.
Ctrl+A	Selects the entire document.

Do it!

B-2: Using the keyboard to select text

Here's how	Here's why
1 Place the insertion point as shown	*About·this·spice* |Also·known·as·" feet·in·its·native·
	You'll use the keyboard to select the paragraph.
2 Press and hold (SHIFT)	
3 Press (→) four times	To select the word "Also."
4 Press (SHIFT) + (END)	To select the first line of the paragraph.
5 Press (SHIFT) + (↓) four times	To select the entire paragraph.
Release (SHIFT)	
6 Deselect the text	

Using the mouse and the selection bar

Explanation

Word has an area called the *selection bar*, which you can use for selecting lines, paragraphs, or an entire document. The selection bar is located on the left side of the document window, in the margin of the page. You'll know when you're in the selection bar because the mouse pointer will change to a right-pointing arrow.

The following table describes techniques for using the selection bar.

To select...	Do this
A line	In the selection bar, point to the line you want to select, and click.
Multiple lines	In the selection bar, point to the first or last line of text you want to select; click and hold the mouse button; drag down or up to the last line of text you want to select; then release the mouse button.
A paragraph	In the selection bar, point to the paragraph and double-click.
The entire document	In the selection bar, point to any line of the document; press and hold Ctrl; and click. You can also triple-click in the selection bar to select the entire document.

B-3: Using the selection bar to select text

Do it!

Here's how	Here's why
1 Move the pointer to the left margin	
	When the pointer is in the selection bar, it becomes a right-pointing arrow.
2 In the selection bar, point to the first line of the paragraph under "About this spice," on page 1	The line begins with "Also known as." The mouse pointer should become a right-pointing arrow.
Click in the selection bar	To select the first line of the paragraph.
3 Double-click the selection bar	To select the entire paragraph.
Deselect the text	
4 Press and hold CTRL	
Click the selection bar	To select the entire document.
Release CTRL	
5 Type **a**	The entire document has been replaced with the letter "a."
6 On the Quick Access toolbar, click	(The Undo button.) To undo the typing.
7 Deselect the text	
8 Close the document without saving	If a dialog box appears, asking whether you want to save the changes, click No.

Unit summary: Navigation and selection techniques

Topic A In this topic, you opened a Word document by using the **Open** dialog box. Then you **navigated** through a document by using the scrollbars, and you **moved** the insertion point by using keyboard commands. You also used the **Go To** command and the **Select Browse Object** button to move to specific parts of a document. You learned how to zoom in and out on a document. Finally, you learned about different **views**, including Print Layout view and Full Screen Reading view.

Topic B In this topic, you **selected text** in various ways. You used the mouse in the document area and in the selection bar, and you used the keyboard.

Independent practice activity

In this activity, you'll open a document. You'll navigate, move the insertion point, and use the Go To command. Then you'll view the document in Full Screen Reading view.

1 Open Spice history (in the current unit folder).
2 Use the scrollbar to navigate through the document.
3 Use the keyboard to move the insertion point to the end of the document.
4 Use the Go To command to go to the first page of the document.
5 View the document in Full Screen Reading view, and then return to Print Layout view.
6 Close the document without saving changes.

Review questions

1 What feature can help you quickly browse graphics in a document?

2 In Print Layout view, how do you hide the white space at the top and bottom of pages?

3 How can you browse two different sections of a document at once?

4 What is an advantage of using Full Screen Reading view instead of Print Layout view?

   A You get a better sense of how the document will look when printed.

   B You can view the text as it would appear in a Web browser.

   C The document is displayed with improved readability because Word automatically scales the text and graphics.

   D You can hide white space.

5 What are the three basic text selection methods?

Unit 3
Editing text

Unit time: 45 minutes

Complete this unit, and you'll know how to:

A Insert and delete text, insert the date and time, and insert symbols and special characters.

B Use the Undo and Redo commands.

C Cut, copy, and paste text.

Topic A: Working with text

This topic covers the following Microsoft Certified Application Specialist exam objective for Word 2007.

#	Objective
1.2.2	**Create and modify headers and footers (Not using Quick Parts)** • Add automatic date and time stamps

Editing documents

Explanation

When you edit a document, you'll likely insert, delete, and format text. Word provides several methods for each action, from deleting individual characters to replacing entire paragraphs or blocks of text.

To add text, place the insertion point where you want the text to appear and start typing. As you type, the characters will appear to the left of the insertion point.

There are various ways to delete text from your documents. The following table shows several techniques.

Press this	To delete this
Backspace	One character to the left of the insertion point. Also moves the insertion point back one space.
Delete	One character to the right of the insertion point, without moving the insertion point.
Ctrl+Delete	All the characters in a word after the insertion point.
Ctrl+Backspace	All the characters in a word before the insertion point.

Editing text **3–3**

Do it! **A-1: Inserting and deleting text**

Here's how	Here's why
1 Open Cookbook letter	From the current unit folder.
Save the document as **My cookbook letter**	In the current unit folder.
2 In the first body paragraph, place the insertion point after "very," as shown	A·word·from·the·chairman¶ ¶ We're·very|·pleased·to·present·expanded·for·2006.¶
	In the first line of the first paragraph under the bold heading.
Press (← BACKSPACE)	To delete the letter "y" from the word "very."
Press (CTRL) + (← BACKSPACE)	To delete the rest of the word and the extra space between "We're" and "pleased."
3 Press (CTRL) + (→)	To move to the beginning of the next word, "pleased."
Press (CTRL) + (→) four more times	To move to the beginning of "edition."
Type **special**	
Press (SPACEBAR)	To insert a space after the word.
4 Move the insertion point to the beginning of **newly**	(Press Ctrl+Right Arrow five times.) On the same line.
Press (DELETE)	To delete the letter "n" from "newly."
Press (CTRL) + (DELETE)	To delete the whole word.
5 Update the document	

Adding the date and time

Explanation

When creating memos and reports, you'll often want to include the date and time. One way to do this is to type the date and time as static text. Sometimes, however, when you update your document, you might forget to also update the date and time. To have the date and time updated automatically when you open a document, you can insert a date-and-time field.

To insert a date-and-time field:

1. Place the insertion point where you want to insert the date and/or time.
2. Activate the Insert tab.
3. In the Text group, click the Date & Time button to open the Date and Time dialog box, shown in Exhibit 3-1.
4. From the Available formats list, select a specific date or time format.
5. If you want the date and time to be updated every time you open the document, check Update automatically. To maintain the date and time as static text, clear this box.
6. Click OK.

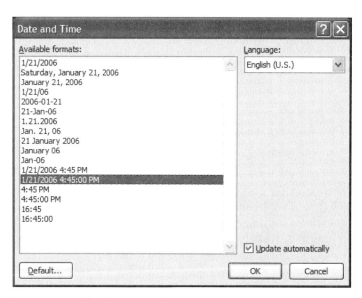

Exhibit 3-1: The Date and Time dialog box

Do it!

A-2: Inserting the date and time

Here's how	Here's why
1 Place the insertion point at the beginning of the document	Press Ctrl+Home.
Type **Draft, last updated on**	You'll insert a field that will display the date and time this document was last updated.
Press SPACEBAR	
2 Activate the Insert tab	
3 In the Text group, click Date & Time	To open the Date and Time dialog box. You'll insert the current date in the document.
Select the indicated date-and-time format	Available formats: 1/21/2006 Saturday, January 21, 2006 January 21, 2006 1/21/06 2006-01-21 21-Jan-06 1.21.2006 Jan. 21, 06 21 January 2006 January 06 Jan-06 1/21/2006 4:45 PM **1/21/2006 4:45:00 PM** 4:45 PM 4:45:00 PM 16:45 16:45:00
	To show the month, day, and year, as well as the hour, minute, and second.
Check **Update automatically**	To have Word update the date and time every time the document is opened.
Click **OK**	To close the dialog box and add the current date and time to the document, in the format you chose.
Observe the date and time	The time is indicated to the second. You'll close and reopen the document to verify that the time is updated.
4 Save and close the document	
5 Open My cookbook letter	The same document you just closed.
Observe the date and time	The time has been updated to indicate the current time, to the second.

Symbols and special characters

Explanation

At times, you might want your document to include symbols and characters—such as currency or copyright symbols—that aren't available on a standard keyboard. Word inserts some symbols automatically. For example, if you type "(c)," Word converts the text to the copyright symbol, "©." Other symbols are available in the Symbol gallery and dialog box.

To insert symbols and special characters:

1. Activate the Insert tab.
2. In the Symbols group, click Symbol to display the Symbol gallery, which displays some commonly used symbols and special characters.
3. Click the symbol or special character you want to insert.

If the symbol or special character isn't available in the Symbol gallery, you can browse the Symbol dialog box. To insert symbols or special characters from the Symbol dialog box:

1. Below the Symbol gallery, choose More Symbols to open the Symbol dialog box.
2. Activate either the Symbols tab or the Special Characters tab.
3. Select the symbol or character you want to insert.
4. In the document, place the insertion point where you want to insert the symbol or character, if necessary.
5. In the dialog box, click Insert.

Editing text **3–7**

Do it! **A-3: Inserting a symbol**

Here's how	Here's why
1 Open PR letter	(From the current unit folder.) You'll add a special character.
Save the document as **My PR letter**	In the current unit folder.
2 In the second paragraph of the memo text, delete **euros**	You'll use the currency symbol instead.
Delete the space between the 9 and the ")" character	If necessary.
3 Place the insertion point as shown	$29.99 (24.99).
	Just after the left parenthesis.
4 Activate the Insert tab	
In the Symbols group, click **Symbol**	To display the Symbol gallery.
Choose **More Symbols…**	To open the Symbol dialog box.
5 From the Subset list, select **Currency Symbols**	(If necessary.) To display the symbols associated with currency.
Select the indicated symbol	
	The euro symbol.
Click **Insert**	To place the symbol at the insertion point's location.
Click **Close**	To close the dialog box.
6 Update and close the document	

Topic B: Using the Undo and Redo commands

Explanation

While working on a document, you might need to go back a few steps—for example, to check an edit you made or to undo a series of actions, such as a deletion and subsequent typing. You can do so by using the Undo command. Or, if needed, you can use the Redo command to repeat an action you undid with the Undo command.

When you don't have any actions to redo, the Redo command becomes the Repeat command. In this case, you can use it to repeat your last action, such as formatting text to a specific style or size.

The Undo command

The Undo command reverses the most recent action you've performed. You can undo an action in two ways:

- Click the Undo button on the Quick Access toolbar.
- Press Ctrl+Z.

Undoing multiple actions

You can also undo several actions at once. To do this, click the down-arrow next to the Undo button to display a list of the actions you've performed since opening the document. In the list, drag to select the actions that you want to undo; when you release the mouse button, Word will undo *all* of the selected actions. (You can't undo an action without also undoing all the previous actions in the list.)

Do it!

B-1: Using the Undo command

Here's how	Here's why
1 In My cookbook letter, delete the last sentence of the fourth body paragraph	This sentence begins, "If you don't see it."
2 Place the insertion point as shown	Inside, you'll find also find some of Just after "Inside," in the second body paragraph.
Press SPACEBAR	
Type **these pages**	
3 Delete the entire third body paragraph	It begins, "We're sure."
Press ←BACKSPACE	To delete the extra paragraph mark.
4 On the Quick Access toolbar, click ↶	(The Undo button.) The extra paragraph mark is reinserted.

5 Click the down-arrow next to the Undo button	To display the Undo list. You can drag to select the actions you want to undo.
Drag to select the two indicated entries; then click	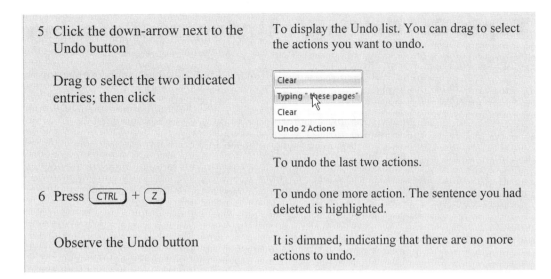
	To undo the last two actions.
6 Press CTRL + Z	To undo one more action. The sentence you had deleted is highlighted.
Observe the Undo button	It is dimmed, indicating that there are no more actions to undo.

The Redo command

Explanation

By using the Redo command, you can reverse the last action you undid. However, you cannot redo multiple actions at once, as you can with the Undo command. Also, the Redo command is available only when you've first undone an action; otherwise, as long as you've typed, edited, or formatted some text, it appears as the Repeat command, as shown in Exhibit 3-2. You can issue the Redo and Repeat commands in two ways:

- Click the Redo or Repeat button on the Quick Access toolbar.
- Press Ctrl+Y.

Exhibit 3-2: The Quick Access toolbar, showing the Redo button (left) and the Repeat button (right)

Do it!

B-2: Using the Redo command

Here's how	Here's why
1 On the Quick Access toolbar, click	(The Redo button.) To delete the last sentence of the fourth paragraph again.
2 Press CTRL + Y	To reinsert the words "these pages" in the second paragraph.
3 Press CTRL + Z	To undo the typing.
4 Update the document	

Topic C: Cutting, copying, and pasting text

This topic covers the following Microsoft Certified Application Specialist exam objective for Word 2007.

#	Objective
2.2.1	**Cut, copy, and paste text** • Cut or copy and paste • Use the Clipboard • Move text • Paste all • Paste one

Rearranging document text

Explanation

In Word, you can move and copy text from one place to another within a document, or to another document altogether. This can save you hours of retyping and ensures consistency within or among documents. If you want to place a selection of text in another location, you can either cut or copy the text.

When you *cut* text, it's completely removed from the original location, but it's still available to be *pasted*, or inserted, in another location—as if you had cut it out of one piece of paper with scissors and were gluing it down on another. When you *copy* text, it remains in its original location and is available to be pasted in another—as if you had photocopied only a specific selection of text.

The Office Clipboard

When you cut or copy text, Word places that text on the Office Clipboard. The *Office Clipboard* is a temporary storage area that holds content so that you can use it again and specify where to place it. Items in the Office Clipboard appear in the Clipboard task pane, shown in Exhibit 3-3. The Office Clipboard can hold up to 24 items. The collected items stay on the Clipboard until you close the Office application, or until you clear them manually.

To display the Clipboard task pane, activate the Home tab; then, in the Clipboard group, click the Dialog Box Launcher. Until you've cut or copied something, the Clipboard is empty. As items are cut or copied from a document, they appear in the Clipboard task pane. The most recent item is listed at the top of the task pane. From this pane, you can paste or delete a single item or all of the items.

To cut text from a document:
1. Select the text you want to move.
2. On the Home tab, in the Clipboard group, click the Cut button, or press Ctrl+X. The text is placed on the Clipboard.

To paste a single item from the Clipboard, place the insertion point in the desired location and click the desired entry in the task pane. You can also click the down-arrow next to the Clipboard item and choose Paste. To paste all of the Clipboard items, click the Paste All button.

To delete a single item, click its down-arrow and choose Delete. To delete all of the Clipboard items, click Clear All.

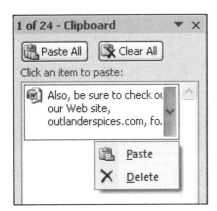

Exhibit 3-3: The Clipboard task pane

The Paste Options button

The text you cut might be formatted differently than the text in the location where you want to paste it. You can choose whether the pasted text should keep its current formatting or inherit the formatting of the destination paragraph. To do this, you use the Paste Options button, which appears to the right of any text you've pasted. Click the Paste Options button to display a drop-down list, and select the desired option.

Do it!

C-1: Moving text and using Paste Options

Here's how	Here's why
1 Activate the Home tab	If necessary.
2 In the Clipboard group, click as shown	(The Dialog Box Launcher.) To display the Clipboard task pane.
3 In the document, select the fourth body paragraph	(Triple-click it.) It begins, "Also, be sure to check out."
4 In the Clipboard group, click	(The Cut button.) Or press Ctrl+X. To cut the selection and add it to the Clipboard.
Press ← BACKSPACE	To delete the extra paragraph return.
5 Place the insertion point as shown	You'll paste the cut text here.
In the Clipboard group, click	(The Paste button.) Or press Ctrl+V. To paste the selection at the insertion point.

6	Observe the Paste Options button	Also, be sure to check well as for ordering in immediate ordering, a down for you.¶ We're sure yo[🗐] find ¶
		The text has been pasted above the insertion point, and the Paste Options button appears below the pasted selection.
	Click the Paste Options button	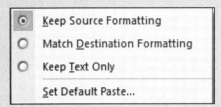
		To display the list of options. By using this list, you can specify how to handle the formatting for the newly pasted text. By default, Keep Source Formatting is selected. You can remove all formatting by selecting Keep Text Only.
	Hide the Paste Options list	(Click the Paste Options button.) To keep the formatting.
7	Press ⏎ ENTER	To insert a paragraph mark after the pasted text.
8	Update the document	

Copying text

Explanation

To copy text to other locations within a document or to different documents, use the Copy and Paste commands. Unlike the Cut command, which moves selected text from one location to another, the Copy command leaves the original text in its original location.

To copy and paste text:

1. Select the text you want to copy.
2. Click the Copy button on the Quick Access toolbar, or press Ctrl+C.
3. Place the insertion point where you want to paste the text.
4. Click the Paste button or press Ctrl+V.

Editing text **3–15**

Do it! **C-2: Copying text from one document to another**

Here's how	Here's why
1 Select the document text, beginning with the heading	Select the heading "A word from the chairman" and all of the text below it.
2 In the Clipboard group, click [icon]	(Or press Ctrl+C.) To copy the text to the Clipboard.
3 Open Cookbook text	(From the current unit folder.) The first page has been left blank so that you can insert the text of the letter you've been working on.
Save the document as **My cookbook text**	In the current unit folder.
4 In the Clipboard task pane, click [Paste All]	(If necessary, click the Dialog Box Launcher in the Clipboard group to display the Clipboard task pane.) To paste all of the Clipboard items into the document. Notice the order in which the items are pasted. They're pasted in reverse order of their listing in the Clipboard task pane.
On the Quick Access toolbar, click [icon] twice	(The Undo button.) To remove the pasted content. Because each item is pasted in succession, and there are two items in the Clipboard, you need to click Undo twice.
5 In the Clipboard task pane, point to the top item	(Don't click it.) When you point to an item in the Clipboard task pane, an arrow appears to its right.
Click as shown	To display a short menu.
Choose **Paste**	To paste the selected text.
6 Update and close all documents	
7 Close the Clipboard task pane	(If necessary.) Click its Close button.

Unit summary: Editing text

Topic A — In this topic, you **inserted** and **deleted** text. Then you used the **Date and Time** dialog box to insert the date and time. Finally, you used the **Symbol** dialog box to insert a symbol.

Topic B — In this topic, you used the **Undo** and **Redo** commands to undo and redo actions. You also learned how to undo multiple actions at once.

Topic C — In this topic, you **moved** and **copied** text within a document. You also used the Paste Options button to specify the formatting of pasted text. In addition, you copied text between documents.

Independent practice activity

In this activity, you'll insert the current date into a document. Then you'll cut and paste some text and insert a special character.

1 Open Practice letter, from the current unit folder, and save it as **My practice letter**.
2 At the top of the letter, insert a date field to display the month, day, and year in a format of your choice.
3 Cut the third paragraph and paste it after the first paragraph.
4 At the bottom of the letter are two comments from Outlander Spices customers. Insert an em dash (—) just before the name of each customer, as shown in Exhibit 3-4. (*Hint*: The em dash is a special character, which you can find in the General Punctuation subset in the Symbol dialog box.)
5 Update and close the document.

The following comments are typical of the letters and e-mails people send us every day:¶

Outlander Spices has been great for my restaurant! Our customers love our new recipes and keep coming back. Thanks!—Bob Gardner, Phila., PA¶

I love to cook, but often felt like I was using spices incorrectly. Thanks to your website and newsletter, I'm always assured the foods I cook taste great! Thanks Outlander Spices!—Jan Salinksy, Dayton, OH¶

Exhibit 3-4: The letter after Step 4 of the independent practice activity

Review questions

1 If you insert a date-and-time field in a document, are the date and time automatically updated to reflect the current date and time?

2 How do you reverse an action?

3 Which of the following is the temporary storage area that holds text until you specify where to place it?

   A Cache

   B Word's Temp folder

   C The Storage task pane

   D Office Clipboard

4 How can you view the contents of the Office Clipboard?

5 What is the difference between cutting text and copying text?

Unit 4
Formatting text

Unit time: 90 minutes

Complete this unit, and you'll know how to:

A Change the appearance of text by applying character formatting.

B Align text by using tabs.

C Format paragraphs by aligning text, adding borders, and applying bullets and numbering.

D Change paragraph indents, line spacing, and paragraph spacing.

E Apply formatting to quotation marks by using AutoFormat.

Topic A: Character formatting

This topic covers the following Microsoft Certified Application Specialist exam objectives for Word 2007.

#	Objective
2.1.1	**Apply styles** • Use Format Painter
2.1.3	**Format characters** • Change fonts • Change font colors • Change font size • Change font case (This objective is also covered in *Word 2007: Intermediate*, in the unit titled "Styles.") • Clear formatting (This objective is also covered in *Word 2007: Intermediate*, in the unit titled "Styles.") • Highlight text • Change character spacing
2.2.1	**Cut, copy, and paste text** • Paste Special

Changing the appearance of text

Explanation

You can draw a reader's attention to specific parts of a document and improve its overall readability by applying character formatting. *Character formats* include fonts, font sizes, and font styles. Although it's not a good idea to use many different formats in a single document, it is generally good practice to use different fonts and text sizes for headlines and body text, for example. Likewise, you might apply italics to indicate emphasis or apply boldface to set off a subheading. Keep in mind that one purpose of character formatting is to draw attention to important information, and too much formatting can make a document difficult to read.

You can apply character formatting by using the various options in the Font dialog box. Many of those options are also available in the Font group, which is on the Home tab. In addition, when you select text, the Mini toolbar appears above it. The Mini toolbar includes some of the formatting options available in the Font and Paragraph groups. The Mini toolbar is shown in Exhibit 4-1.

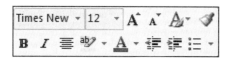

Exhibit 4-1: Formatting options available on the Mini toolbar

Fonts and font sizes

The font and size of text can greatly affect its readability, and different kinds of fonts are typically used for different purposes. For example, an elegant script font would be appropriate for a wedding invitation but not for a business letter. Two commonly used fonts are Times New Roman and Arial. Word 2007 uses Calibri as the default font for new documents.

The design of a set of characters is called a *font*. (Sometimes "font" and "typeface" are used interchangeably, but traditionally, a font is actually the combination of typeface, type style, and type size.) Fonts can be categorized in various ways, such as by their typical use or by certain design characteristics. Two categories based on the latter are serif and sans serif.

A *serif* font has small lines at the top and bottom of its letters. (Think of them as small feet at the bottom of the letters.) For example, the font used in the paragraph below the heading in Exhibit 4-2 is a serif font—Times New Roman. A serif font works well on a printed page with large blocks of text because the lines help lead the reader's eyes across the page.

A *sans serif* font lacks the small lines of a serif font. For example, the heading, "A word from the chairman," in Exhibit 4-2 uses a sans serif font—Arial. A sans serif font works well for headings because the streamlined letter shapes make the text easy to read at a glance.

> **A word from the chairman**
>
> We're excited to present this edition of Outlander Cooking!, revised and expanded for 2006.

Exhibit 4-2: A heading using a sans serif font with a bold style, and body text using a serif font

Font styles

Font styles (also called *type styles*) include italic, bold, and underlined. You can emphasize a specific word or phrase by using these styles. For example, using boldface text in headings, like the one shown in Exhibit 4-2, helps draw a reader's attention to important information. In addition, the bold heading format helps the reader see the document's sections and structure, making it easier to read and process.

One way to apply font styles is to select the desired text and use the Bold, Italic, or Underline buttons in the Font group. You can also apply these font styles by using the keyboard. The following table shows the font styles and the Ribbon buttons and keys used to apply them.

Style	Button	Keyboard shortcut
Bold	**B**	Ctrl+B
Italic	*I*	Ctrl+I
Underline	U	Ctrl+U

Removing font styles

There might be times when you want to remove any extra styles from text. To remove all styles applied to text, select the text and press Ctrl+Spacebar.

Do it! **A-1: Applying character formatting**

Here's how	Here's why
1 Open Cookbook	(From the current unit folder.) You'll improve the formatting in this document.
Save the document as **My cookbook**	In the current unit folder.
2 Using the mouse, select the heading on page 1, and then point to the selection	("A word from the chairman.") The Mini toolbar appears above the selection.
3 On the Mini toolbar, click **B**	To apply the bold format.
4 In the Font group, click the Font list	(On the Home tab.) To display the list of available fonts.
Point to a font name	To highlight it in the list.
Observe the text you've selected in the document	As you point to a font in the Font list, the selected text is displayed in that font.
From the font list, select **Trebuchet MS**	You might need to scroll through the list.
5 In the Font group, from the Font Size list, select **24**	As you point to each font size in the Font Size list, the selected text is displayed in that size.

6	Click as shown	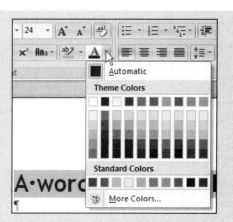
		To display the Font Color gallery.
	Select the indicated color	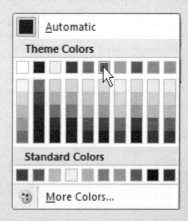
		(Red, Accent 2.) Again, as you point to each color swatch, you see a preview of that color applied to the selected text.
7	Place the insertion point as shown	
		In the first line of the first paragraph.
	Press CTRL + SHIFT + →	To select the word "Outlander."
	Press CTRL + SHIFT + →	To select the word "Cooking."
	Press SHIFT + →	To select the exclamation point.
8	In the Font group, click *I*	(The Italic button.) To format text in italics.
	Deselect the text	To observe the formatting.
9	Update the document	

The Font dialog box

Explanation

You can also use the Font dialog box to apply character formats. The Font dialog box offers several additional options, such as underline style, underline color, character effects, and character spacing.

As with font styles, you'll want to apply character effects judiciously to specific text that you want to highlight. For example, you might apply a drop shadow to a headline, but a large block of text with a drop shadow applied to it would be difficult to read and visually unappealing.

You can use the Character Spacing tab in the Font dialog box to change the distance between letters in the selected text.

To change letter spacing or apply character effects to text:

1. Select the text you want to format.
2. In the Font group, click the Dialog Box Launcher to open the Font dialog box, shown in Exhibit 4-3.
3. Under Effects, check the options you want to apply.
4. Use the Character Spacing tab to change the letter spacing, if desired.
5. Under Preview, observe a preview of the effects applied to the selection. When you're satisfied with the results of your settings, click OK.

Hidden text

You already know that Word inserts nonprinting characters, such as paragraph marks and tab characters. In addition, you can format any text that you type as hidden—it won't appear in the document unless you click the Show/Hide button to display nonprinting characters or check "Hidden text" in the Word Options dialog box. To format text as hidden, select it, and in the Font dialog box, check Hidden.

The default font

When you create a new document, Word uses the Calibri font for body text by default. To change the default font, open the Font dialog box. Select the desired font from the Font list, select any formatting options you want to use, and click Default.

Exhibit 4-3: The Font dialog box

Do it!

A-2: Using the Font dialog box

Here's how	Here's why
1 Move to the top of page 2	
2 Select the heading	"Contents."
3 In the Font group, click the Dialog Box Launcher, as shown	To open the Font dialog box, which provides more options for formatting text.
From the Font list, select **Trebuchet MS**	
From the Font style list, select **Bold**	
From the Size list, select **24**	
From the Font color list, select **Red, Accent 2**	The same color you applied to the heading on page 1.
4 Under Effects, check **Shadow**	To apply a drop shadow to the text.
Check **Small caps**	To apply the small-caps effect to the text.
Observe the Preview section	
	The text looks a bit cramped. You'll increase the spacing between characters.
5 Activate the Character Spacing tab	
From the Spacing list, select **Expanded**	
Edit the By box to read **2 pt**	
6 Click **OK**	To close the dialog box and apply the formatting to the selected text.
Deselect and observe the text	
7 Update the document	

Using the Highlight tool

Explanation

You can draw attention to specific text by highlighting it with a different color. You can do this by clicking the down-arrow next to the Text Highlight Color button in the Font group and selecting a color.

There are two ways to use this tool:

- One-time use:
    1. Select the text you want to highlight.
    2. Click the Text Highlight Color button. The highlighting is applied, and the tool is turned off automatically.
- Multiple uses:
    1. Click the Text Highlight Color button.
    2. Select the text you want to highlight.
    3. Continue to select text to highlight it. The tool remains active until you turn it off by clicking the Text Highlight Color button again or by pressing Esc.

Do it! **A-3: Highlighting text**

Here's how	Here's why
1 Select the indicated line	You'll highlight the selected text.
2 In the Font group, click as shown	(The down-arrow on the Text Highlight Color button.) To display the Text Highlight Color gallery.
Select **Gray-25%**	To highlight the text. This color will remain on the Highlight button until you choose a different color.
3 Apply the same highlight color to the next line	(The line begins, "Spice descriptions.") Select the text and click the Text Highlight Color button. After you apply the highlighting, Word automatically deselects the text.
4 Click the Text Highlight Color button again	To activate it. Now, any text you select will be highlighted with the gray color.
Select the **Recipes** line	To highlight it.
5 Click the Text Highlight Color button	To deactivate it.
6 Update the document	

Repeating character formatting

Explanation

At times, you might want to repeat certain character formatting in several parts of a document. If you've just applied formatting, you can use Word's Repeat command to apply that formatting to other text in the document. This option is especially useful when you're using the Font dialog box, because you can apply several formats to one text selection, and then repeat the formatting for other text throughout the document.

To repeat font formatting that you've just applied, you can click the Repeat button on the Quick Access toolbar or press F4.

Using the Format Painter to apply character formatting

Word provides another option, the Format Painter, for repeating formatting in a document. The Format Painter copies the formatting of text and applies it to other text you select. This tool can save time if you're working with a document that you've already partially formatted. For example, if you like the format of a heading, you can use the Format Painter to copy the format to all other headings in the document.

To repeat formatting by using the Format Painter:

1. Select the text that has the formatting you want to copy.
2. Click the Format Painter button.
3. Select the text you want to format.

Do it!

A-4: Using the Format Painter

Here's how	Here's why
1 Move to page 3	
2 Select the subheading **Spices as ancient medicine**	
Underline the text	Click the Underline button on the Mini toolbar or in the Font group.
3 Open the Font Color gallery	In the Font group, click the down-arrow next to the Font Color button.
Below the Olive Green, Accent 3, select **Olive Green, Accent 3, Darker 50%**	To select the text color.
4 In the Clipboard group, click	(The Format Painter button.) The pointer changes to a paintbrush. You'll use this to copy the subheading's new formatting.
5 Scroll to the bottom of page 3	If necessary.
Select the subheading **Spices as modern medicine**	To apply the underlining and color formatting to it.
6 Apply the formatting to the subheading on page 4	Select the text. The Format Painter button will be automatically deselected after the formatting is applied.
7 Update the document	

Using Paste Special to copy text without formatting

Explanation

There might be times when you'd like to copy text from one location to another, but do not want to copy its formatting. When you need more pasting options, you can use the Paste Special command.

To copy text without the formatting:

1. Select the text and copy it to the Clipboard.
2. Place the insertion point where you'd like the text be duplicated.
3. On the Home tab, in the Clipboard group, click the lower portion of the Paste button to display a menu.
4. Choose Paste Special to open the Paste Special dialog box, which provides additional options.
5. Verify that Paste is selected on the left.
6. Under As, select Unformatted Text.
7. Click OK.

Do it!

A-5: Using Paste Special

Here's how	Here's why
1 Select the subheading **The spice trade**, as shown	*The spice trade* ¶ On page 4.
2 Press CTRL + C	To copy the formatted text to the Clipboard.
3 Place the insertion point at the beginning of the first paragraph below the subheadings	*The spice trade* ¶ ¶ *A funny thing happe* ¶ |has driven a good d a slew of explorers t The line beginning with "has driven a good deal."
4 Click as shown	[Paste icon] To display a menu.
5 Choose **Paste Special…**	To open the Paste Special dialog box.
Under As, select **Unformatted Text**	
Click **OK**	To paste the contents of the Clipboard as unformatted text.
6 Update the document	

Topic B: Tab settings

This topic covers the following Microsoft Certified Application Specialist exam objective for Word 2007.

#	Objective
2.1.5	**Set and clear tabs** • Tabs with leaders • Clear one tab • Clear all tabs

Using tabs to organize text

Explanation

You can use tabs to align text. *Tab stops* are positions set on the horizontal ruler for the purpose of aligning text. Each time you press Tab, any text to the right of the insertion point moves to the first tab stop on the ruler. Tabs can be helpful for aligning columns of text.

Five types of tab stops are available. Each one has a different effect on text when you press Tab. The five tab types are described in the following table.

Tab	Description
Left	Aligns the left edge of text with the tab stop.
Center	Centers text under the tab stop.
Right	Aligns the right edge of text with the tab stop.
Decimal	Aligns any decimal point under the tab stop.
Bar	Automatically inserts a vertical line under the tab stop.

Do it!

B-1: Examining tab stops

Here's how	Here's why
1 Open Tabs	(From the current unit folder. The My cookbook file remains open.) Five types of tabs are set in this document.
2 At the top of the vertical scrollbar, click	(The View Ruler button.) To show the ruler.
3 Click within **Left tab**	In the first paragraph.
Observe the ruler at the 3" mark	This is the Left Tab indicator. The left edge of the text aligns with the tab stop.
4 Click within **Center tab**	The second block of text.
Observe the ruler at the 3" mark	This is the Center Tab indicator. The text is centered under the tab stop.
5 Click within **Right tab**	
Observe the ruler	This is the Right Tab indicator. The right edge of the text is aligned with the tab stop.
6 Click within **1.23**	This is the Decimal Tab indicator. The numbers are aligned on the decimal point.
7 Click within **Bar tab**	The middle tab stop shown here is the Bar tab indicator. A vertical line divides the text at the 3" mark.
8 Close the document without saving	

Setting custom tabs

Explanation

By default, tab stops are set every half inch on the horizontal ruler. You can, however, set your own tab stops; this process clears the default tab stops to the left of those that you set manually. Setting your own tabs helps, for example, when you're creating headings for a memo or lining up text in a table.

You can set tabs by using the Tab Alignment button on the far left side of the ruler. By default, the Tab Alignment button sets a left tab. To choose one of the other tab types, click the button until you see the tab type you want.

To set a custom tab stop on the ruler:

1. Display the ruler, if necessary.
2. Select the paragraphs for which you want to set tabs.
3. Click the Tab Alignment button to select the type of tab you want to use.
4. On the ruler, click the position where you want to place the tab stop.

Moving custom tabs

You can move a custom tab stop by dragging it to a new location on the ruler. (First, select the paragraphs whose tab stop you want to move.) Because the tabbed text moves along with the tab stop, you can immediately see how the change will affect the text.

Do it!

B-2: Setting and moving a custom tab stop

Here's how	Here's why
1 Open PR letter	From the current unit folder.
Save the document as **My PR letter**	In the current unit folder.
2 Place the insertion point after **Date:**	At the end of the line.
3 Press `TAB` twice	
Observe the horizontal ruler	The default tab stops are set every half-inch.
4 Press `← BACKSPACE`	To delete one of the tab characters.
5 Use the Date & Time button to insert the current date	(Activate the Insert tab; click the Date & Time button in the Text group; select a format; and click OK.) To add the current date to the document.
6 Select the indicated paragraphs	Outlander·Spices™¶ Date:→2/7/2006¶ To: → Outlander·Spices·employees¶ From:→Ann·Salinski¶ Re: → Internal·update¶ ¶
Point as shown	
	(But do not click.) The Tab Alignment button on the ruler is set for a left tab.
7 Click at 2" on the horizontal ruler	To set a left-aligned tab stop at 2". The left edge of the text aligns with the tab stop at 2".
Drag the tab stop to 0.75"	
8 Deselect the text and observe the document	The text moved to the new tab-stop position.
9 Update the document	

Clearing custom tabs

Explanation — You can clear any or all custom tab stops. To do so, select the paragraph to be affected, and drag the tab indicator off the ruler and into the text area. When all custom tab stops are cleared, the default tab stops are automatically reset to every half-inch on the ruler.

Do it!

B-3: Clearing and setting other types of tabs

Here's how	Here's why
1 Select the indicated lines	Outlander Spices™¶ Date: → 2/7/2006¶ To: → Outlander Spices employees¶ From: → Ann Salinski¶ Re: → Internal update¶ ¶
2 Point to the custom tab stop at 0.75"	The tab stop you set.
Drag the tab stop down and off of the ruler	To delete the custom tab stop. Word reverts to the default tabs, set every half-inch.
3 Select the indicated text	The cookbook will be available in book stores and directly from our Web site. In addition, we'll be selling it at our kiosks located throughout the country. We'll stock kiosks based on revenue, as shown in the following table.¶ State → City → Store Location → Cookbooks¶ MD → Baltimore → Prestige Market → 112¶ MD → Bethesda → Prestige Market → 175¶ MD → Rockville → Mediterranean Gourmet → 80¶ NJ → Cherry Hill → Patterson's Grocers → 180¶ NJ → Trenton → Roma → 75¶ NY → Albany → Prestige Market → 95¶ NY → Buffalo → Mediterranean Gourmet → 60¶ NY → New York → Patterson's Grocers → 215¶ NY → New York → Village Gourmet Bakery → 230¶ PA → Harrisburg → Patterson's Grocers → 140¶ PA → Philadelphia → Patterson's Grocers → 165¶ VA → Charlottesville → Roma → 120¶ VA → Fairfax → Mediterranean Gourmet → 110¶ Closing¶ We've all put in many hours of hard work to complete this project. Thanks to everyone who had had a hand in seeing this through. Next year's cookbook is sure to be even better!¶ You might need to scroll the document.
4 Remove the custom tab stop at 4.75"	(Drag the rightmost custom tab stop off of the horizontal ruler.) You'll add a right tab to align the numbers.
5 Click [L]	[⊥] (The Tab Alignment button on the ruler.) When you click the button, it changes to a Center tab button.
Click [⊥]	[⌐] The Tab Alignment button changes to a Right tab button.
6 Click at 5.25" on the horizontal ruler	To set a right tab stop at 5.25". The numbers align under the tab stop.
7 Update the document	

Using the Tabs dialog box to clear tabs

Explanation

By using the Tabs dialog box, you can clear a single tab or all tabs in the selected paragraph. To open the dialog box, click Tabs in the Paragraph dialog box.

To delete a single tab by using the Tabs dialog box:

1. In the Tabs dialog box, under Tab stop position, select the tab you want to delete.
2. Click Clear.
3. Click OK.

To delete all tabs from the selected paragraph, open the Tabs dialog box, click Clear All, and click OK.

Do it!

B-4: Clearing all tabs

Here's how	Here's why
1 Select the indicated text	[image of cookbook table text]
	If necessary.
2 In the Paragraph group, click the Dialog Box Launcher	(On the Home tab.) To open the Paragraph dialog box.
3 Click **Tabs**	To open the Tabs dialog box.
4 Under Tab stop positions, observe the list of custom tabs that have been set	Custom tabs are set at 1.25", 2.5", and 5.25".
5 Click **Clear All**	To remove all custom tab stops from the selected paragraphs. Notice that the list of custom tabs under Tab stop positions is empty.
Click **OK**	To close the Tabs dialog box and view the document.
6 Observe the tabbed table	The custom tabs have been removed.
7 Undo the Clear All command	On the Quick Access toolbar, click Undo.

Adding tab leaders

Explanation

By using the Tabs dialog box, shown in Exhibit 4-4, you can specify exact positions on the ruler that are difficult to set with the mouse. For example, if you want to set a tab stop at 4.18", you can type 4.18 in the Tab stop position box in the Tabs dialog box. The disadvantage of this technique is that you have to exit the dialog box to see the effect of the tab stop.

You can also use the Tabs dialog box to add a leader to a tab. A *leader* is a series of characters (such as dots or dashes) that fill in the spaces between tabbed text. Dot leaders are commonly used in tables of contents.

Exhibit 4-4: The Tabs dialog box

Do it!

B-5: Setting a tab and leader in the Tabs dialog box

Here's how	Here's why
1 Go to the My cookbook document	Use the Windows taskbar.
2 Move to page 2	The Contents page.
3 Select the first two lines of text under "Contents"	"The long history of spices" and "Spice descriptions."
Press CTRL and select the **Recipes** line	To select all three lines at once.
4 Activate the Home tab	If necessary.
Open the Paragraph dialog box	In the Paragraph group, click the Dialog Box Launcher.
Click **Tabs**	(In the lower-left corner of the dialog box.) To open the Tabs dialog box. Here, you can specify a position for tab stops, as well as choose an alignment option and a leader.

5 In the Tab stop position box, enter **5**	To set a new tab at the 5" mark.
Under Alignment, select **Right**	
Under Leader, select **2**	To choose a dot leader.
Click **OK**	You've set a right-aligned tab stop at 5" and added a dot leader. Now you'll add another tab stop that sets off the sections under "Spice descriptions."
6 Select the remaining lines	Select the "Bay leaf" through "Turmeric" lines; then press Ctrl and select the "Spicy Buzzard Wings" through "Wasabi Pork Tenderloin" lines.
	You'll create two tab stops for this text because you want it to be indented relative to the page headings.
7 Open the Tabs dialog box	In the Paragraph dialog box, click Tabs.
In the Tab stop position box, enter **1**	
Click **Set**	To add the tab stop without closing the dialog box.
Create a right-aligned tab stop at 5" with a dot leader	Edit the Tab stop position box to read 5; under Alignment, select Right; under Leader, select 2. Then click Set.
Click **OK**	To close the dialog box and apply the tab stops.
8 Deselect the text	
9 Update the document	

Topic C: Paragraph formatting

This topic covers the following Microsoft Certified Application Specialist exam objectives for Word 2007.

#	Objective
2.1.4	**Format paragraphs** • Change alignment
4.2.1	**Create tables and lists** (This objective is also covered in the unit titled "Creating tables.") • Convert text to lists
4.2.2	**Sort content** • Sort list items
4.2.3	**Modify list formats** • Change numbering options • Change bullet options • Promote and demote list items

Formatting options

Explanation

You can apply several types of formatting to paragraphs. For example, you can change their alignment, add bullets and numbers to create bulleted and numbered lists, and add borders and shading. Before you apply a format, you need to select the paragraphs you want to apply it to.

Selecting paragraphs

Unlike with character formatting, when you apply paragraph formatting, you usually don't need to select an entire paragraph. Instead, to select a single paragraph, just click anywhere inside it. To select multiple paragraphs, select a part of each paragraph.

Repeating and copying paragraph formatting

If you've just applied paragraph formatting and you want to apply it to another paragraph, you can use the Repeat command (press F4 or click the Repeat button). You can also use the Format Painter to copy formatting to other paragraphs. To copy paragraph formatting with the Format Painter, you must select the entire paragraph, including the paragraph mark.

Paragraph alignment

One type of paragraph formatting that you'll probably use often is alignment. When you apply left or right alignment, paragraphs are aligned along their left or right indents. By default, these are the same as the left and right margins of a page. *Margins* define the space at the top, bottom, and sides of a document.

The four paragraph-alignment options are Align Text Left, Center, Align Text Right, and Justify. You can apply them by using the alignment buttons in the Paragraph group (or by using the Paragraph dialog box). The following table describes these options.

Alignment	Button	Description
Left		The text is lined up evenly along the left side of the paragraph. The right side is *ragged*, which means that it's uneven.
Center		The text is centered on the page or within the paragraph's indents. Both the left and right sides are ragged.
Right		The text is lined up evenly on the right side, and the left side is ragged.
Justify		The text is lined up evenly on both the left and right sides. Word adjusts the spacing between letters and words in each line (except the last line).

Do it!

C-1: Changing paragraph alignment

Here's how	Here's why
1 Move to page 1	In the My cookbook document.
2 Place the insertion point anywhere in the second paragraph	(It begins, "Inside, you'll find.") You don't need to select the entire paragraph to apply paragraph formatting to it.
3 Observe the Alignment buttons in the Paragraph group	
	(On the Home tab.) The Align Text Left button is selected.
Click	(The Align Text Right button.) The paragraph is now right-aligned.
Click	(The Center button.) The paragraph is centered on page 1.
Click	(The Justify button.) The spacing between words is adjusted so that the lines of text (except for the last one) line up evenly along the left and right margins.
4 Apply Justified alignment to the body-text paragraphs on this page	Select from the paragraph beginning "We're excited" through the one beginning "P.S." Then click the Justify button.
5 Update the document	

Borders and shading

Explanation

You can add borders around paragraphs to set them apart from the remaining text. For example, a heading is an important part of a report. You can add interest or emphasis to a heading by adding a border around it and shading it with a suitable color.

To add borders and shading, first select a paragraph. Then, on the Home tab, in the Paragraph group, click the Borders button, and select a border style from the menu.

The Borders and Shading dialog box

To set additional options for borders and shading, display the Border menu and choose Borders and Shading. This opens the Borders and Shading dialog box, shown in Exhibit 4-5.

To use the Borders and Shading dialog box to specify border settings:

1. Select an option under Setting: None, Box, Shadow, 3-D, or Custom.
2. Select a style, color, and width for the border.
3. In the Preview section, you can choose settings for specific parts of the border. To do so:
   a. Under Setting, click Custom.
   b. Specify a style, color, and width.
   c. In the Preview section, click the border area that you want to apply those settings to.
   d. Continue specifying custom settings and applying them to areas of the border as necessary.
4. Click OK.

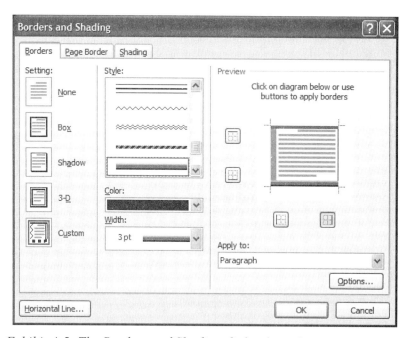

Exhibit 4-5: The Borders and Shading dialog box, showing custom settings

Formatting text **4–25**

Do it! **C-2: Applying borders and shading**

Here's how	Here's why
1 Select the heading on page 1	"A word from the chairman."
2 In the Paragraph group, click as shown	(The down-arrow on the Shading button.) To open the Shading gallery.
Under Theme Colors, select the indicated color swatch	(The Olive Green, Accent 3, Lighter 40% swatch.) To format the selected text with a shaded background.
3 Click as shown	(The down-arrow on the Borders button.) To display the Borders menu.
Choose **Outside Borders**	To apply a border to the outside of the selected text.
4 Deselect the text	To observe the formatting.
5 Update the document	

Inserting bulleted and numbered lists

Explanation

You might want to group information so that important sections stand out or are easier to read. You can organize and draw attention to lists by adding bullets and numbers.

To quickly add bullets or numbering to a list, first select the paragraph you want to affect. Then, in the Paragraph group on the Home tab, click the Bullets, Numbering, or Multilevel List buttons. For more options, click the down-arrow next to each button to display a gallery of bullet and number formats.

After you've formatted a bulleted or numbered list, Word automatically updates the list when you add items to it. For example, if you press Enter after the second item in a numbered list with seven items, Word creates a new item number three and renumbers the subsequent items in the list. To add a sub-item to a list, press Tab.

Do it!

C-3: Adding bulleted and numbered lists

Here's how	Here's why
1 Move to page 5	"Bay leaf" appears at the top of this page.
2 Scroll down to see the bulleted list	(Located under "How to use this spice.") You'll apply similar formatting to another list.
3 Move to page 12	The Star anise section.
4 Select the indicated text	meat and poultry¶ Chinese stocks and soups¶ fruit compotes¶ jams¶ Under "How to use this spice."
In the Paragraph group, click	(The Bullets button.) To apply bullets to each paragraph in the selected text.
5 Move to page 14	
6 Select the indicated text	The recipe directions. Preheat oven to 425°.¶ In a bowl, mix paprika, caraway seeds, onion flakes, dry mustard, thyme leaves, salt and ground red pepper.¶ With hands, lightly pat paprika mixture on chicken wings.¶ Brush chicken wings with Buzzard's Best® Hot Wing Sauce.¶ Place chicken wings in a large baking dish.¶ Bake 30 minutes or until chicken wings are fork-tender.¶ Place chicken wings on platter. Garnish with celery.¶
In the Paragraph group, click	(The Numbering button.) To sequentially number the items in the list.
7 Update the document	

Modifying bulleted and numbered lists

Explanation

You can use the Bullets and Numbering galleries to apply and modify the bullet and numbering styles. In addition, you can change the format of the bullets and numbers in a list without affecting the text in the list. For example, you can change the color of bullets and make them bold while leaving the formatting of the list text intact. To do so, select one bullet or number in a list and apply formatting options; any formatting you apply will be applied to all of the bullets or numbers in the list.

You can use any picture, symbol, or font as a bullet. To use a picture as a bullet:

1. Select the bulleted list to be affected.
2. In the Bullets gallery, choose Define New Bullet to open the Define New Bullet dialog box.
3. Click Picture to open the Picture Bullet dialog box, shown in Exhibit 4-6.
4. Select a bullet icon in the dialog box, or click Import to use any picture from your hard drive.
5. Click OK to close the Picture Bullet dialog box.
6. Click OK to apply the bullet and to close the Define New Bullet dialog box.

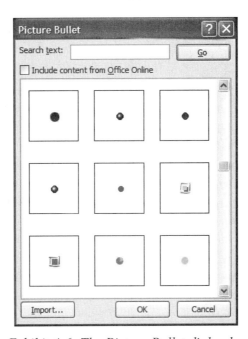

Exhibit 4-6: The Picture Bullet dialog box

Promoting and demoting list items

You can increase or decrease the indentation of list items to create sub-lists. To do this, you can use the Increase Indent and Decrease Indent buttons, which are in the Paragraph group on the Home tab.

The Increase Indent button shifts the selected list items one level to the right. If you click the Increase Indent button a second time, the text is indented another level to the right. Conversely, the Decrease Indent button shifts the selected items one level to the left each time you click it. If you're modifying a numbered list, the numbering scheme is automatically updated when you use these commands.

Sorting list items

You can alphabetize list items by using the Sort Text dialog box. You can sort using up to three levels of criteria, and you can specify the sort order (ascending or descending). To sort a list:

1. Select the list you want to alphabetize.
2. On the Home tab, in the Paragraph group, click Sort to open the Sort Text dialog box.
3. Specify your sorting criteria.
4. Click OK.

Do it!

C-4: Editing bulleted and numbered lists

Here's how	Here's why
1 Move to page 12	
Drag to select the text of the bulleted list	[list showing: meat and poultry, Chinese stocks and soups, fruit compotes, jams] The list under "How to use this spice."
2 In the Paragraph group, click [A-Z Sort button]	(The Sort button.) To open the Sort Text dialog box.
Observe the settings	You can specify up to three levels of sorting criteria. By default, the text of each bulleted item will be sorted in ascending order (alphabetical order). You'll use these default settings.
Click **OK**	To sort the bulleted list in alphabetical order.
3 Open the Bullets gallery	Click the down-arrow on the Bullets button.
Select a bullet of your choice	To replace the default bullet.
4 In the bulleted list, click the first bullet	[list showing: Chinese stocks and soups, fruit compotes, jams, meat and poultry] (Your bullet shape might not be the same as the one pictured here.) Select only the bullet, not the text.
5 Change the bullet's color to Red, Accent 2, Lighter 40%	Open the Font Color gallery, and select the Red, Accent 2, Lighter 40% swatch.
Deselect the bullets	The bullets are olive green, but the text is unchanged.

6	Select the numbered list on page 14	The numbered steps in the recipe.
7	Open the Numbering gallery	Click the down-arrow on the Numbering button.
	Select a numbering scheme of your choice	To replace the default numbering.
8	Place the insertion point in the text of the second item in the numbered list	The item beginning with "In a bowl, mix."
	In the Paragraph group, click ![indent]	(The Increase Indent button.) To increase the indentation of the second item in the list.
	Observe the numbering of the second item	It's automatically updated to a second-level numbering scheme.
9	Verify that the second item is still selected	
	In the Paragraph group, click ![indent]	(The Decrease Indent button.) To decrease the indent.
	Update the document	

Topic D: Paragraph spacing and indents

This topic covers the following Microsoft Certified Application Specialist exam objective for Word 2007.

#	Objective
2.1.4	**Format paragraphs** • Change line spacing • Change paragraph spacing • Change indentation

Indenting text

Explanation

You can set off blocks of text by using indents. *Indents* define the left and right sides of a paragraph relative to the margins of the page. By default, indents are set to match the left and right margins; that is, the indents are set to zero, so paragraphs stretch from the left margin to the right one.

You can set indents by using the Paragraph dialog box, the Paragraph group on the Page Layout tab, or the ruler. The ruler contains four indent markers, as shown in Exhibit 4-7. The following table describes these markers and their uses.

Item	Description
First Line Indent	The down-pointing triangle on the left side of the ruler. Use this marker to control the left indent for the first line of a paragraph.
Hanging Indent	The up-pointing triangle on the left side of the ruler. Use this marker to control the left indent of all lines in a paragraph *except* the first line.
Left Indent	The box under the hanging-indent triangle. Use this marker to control the left indent for an entire paragraph.
Right Indent	The up-pointing triangle on the right side of the ruler. Use this marker to control the right indent of a paragraph.

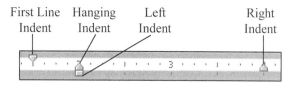

Exhibit 4-7: Indent markers on the ruler

Formatting text **4–31**

To set indents, you can drag the indent markers to new locations on the ruler. To set a new left or right indent for every line in a paragraph:

1. Click in the paragraph you want to indent, or, if there's more than one paragraph, select a part of each one.
2. On the ruler, drag the left indent or right indent marker to the indent position you want to apply.

In addition, you can set indents by selecting paragraphs and pressing Tab. If you select the first line of a paragraph and press Tab, Word creates a first-line indent set at 0.5". If you select any other line of the paragraph and press Tab, Word indents the entire paragraph 0.5"; Word indents the paragraph another 0.5" every time you press Tab.
Note: For this method to work, the "Set left- and first-indent with tabs and backspaces" option must be checked on the AutoFormat As You Type tab in the AutoCorrect dialog box.

Do it!

D-1: Setting indents

Here's how	Here's why
1 Move to page 1	
2 Display the ruler	(If necessary,) At the top of the vertical scrollbar, click the View Ruler button.
3 Click in the first paragraph below the heading	The left and right indent markers are set at the document's margins.
4 Drag the left indent marker to **0.5"**	The paragraph is indented.
5 Set the left indent for all of the text on this page to **0.5"**	(Include the heading.) Select the text and drag the left indent marker.
6 Apply a 0.5" right indent to all of the text on this page	(Include the heading.) Select the text, if necessary, and drag the right indent marker 0.5" to the left.
7 Move to page 3	The first line of the second body paragraph should be indented.
8 Select the first line of the second body paragraph	(Point to the line on the selection bar and click.) Under the subheading "Introduction," the line begins "In the pages that follow."
Press `TAB`	To indent only the first line.
9 Update the document	

Hanging indents

Explanation

A *hanging indent* is a paragraph with the first line indented to the left of the rest of the paragraph; all of the lines below the first appear to "hang" below the first. Hanging indents are typically used in numbered lists, such as the numbered steps in this book's hands-on activities. Hanging indents might also be used in such reference lists as bibliographical citations in endnotes.

To set a hanging indent, select the paragraph (or paragraphs) you want to affect, and then drag the first-line indent marker to the left of the hanging-indent marker on the ruler. (You can also use the Paragraph dialog box.)

Creating a new line instead of a new paragraph

When you press Enter to start a new paragraph, the new paragraph begins at the first-line indent marker. When you're working with paragraphs with hanging indents, however, you might want to start a new line at the hanging-indent marker. To do that, you can enter a line break instead of a paragraph mark. (You can enter line breaks in any kind of paragraph, not just those with hanging indents.)

To insert a manual line break, creating a new line without starting a new paragraph, press Shift+Enter.

Do it!

D-2: Setting a hanging indent

Here's how	Here's why
1 Open Works cited	From the current unit folder.
	This document contains a list of sources used when preparing the information in the cookbook. You'll format them with hanging indents.
Save the document as **My works cited**	
2 Select the two paragraphs under the heading "Works cited"	
3 Open the Paragraph dialog box	
4 Under Indentation, from the Special list, select **Hanging**	
Observe the By box	The default value for a hanging indent is 0.5". You'll use the default.
5 Click **OK**	To close the dialog box. The citations are formatted with hanging indents.
6 Update and close the document	

Paragraph and line spacing

Explanation

Another way to improve the readability and impact of your documents is to set line spacing and paragraph spacing. *Line spacing* controls the amount of vertical space between the lines of a paragraph. *Paragraph spacing* controls the amount of vertical space between paragraphs. You can set both types of spacing by using the Paragraph dialog box. Additionally, you can set line spacing by using tools in the Paragraph group on the Home tab, and set paragraph spacing by using tools in the Paragraph group on the Page Layout tab.

Setting space before and after paragraphs

When you create a new, blank document, Word automatically sets paragraphs to have a 10-point space after them. You might, however, want to adjust the space above or below paragraphs to make text easier to read or for space considerations. Adding space in this way gives you more control over spacing between paragraphs than does adding paragraph returns manually.

To use the Ribbon to change the amount of space before or after a paragraph, activate the Page Layout tab. Then, in the Paragraph group, edit the values in the Before and After boxes.

Do it!

D-3: Setting the spacing after a paragraph

Here's how	Here's why
1 In My cookbook, move to the beginning of page 3	If necessary.
2 Select the first two body paragraphs	After the Introduction subheading.
3 Activate the Page Layout tab	
Observe the Paragraph group	You can use it to set indents and paragraph spacing.
4 Under Spacing, edit the Spacing After box to read **6 pt**	The spacing below each paragraph increases to 6 points.
5 Select the three body paragraphs under the subheading "The medicinal use of spices"	The first paragraph begins, "The people who first."
Press [F4]	To repeat the formatting. The Spacing After formatting is applied to each paragraph.
6 Apply the formatting to the body paragraphs on page 4	Select the paragraphs and press F4, or edit the value in the Spacing After box.
7 Update the document	

Line spacing

Explanation

Line spacing is set at Single (1.0) by default. Increasing the line spacing can sometimes improve readability, especially for long lines of text. It can also be useful if you know that other people will be editing the document on paper and will need room to write between the lines.

You can set line spacing by using the Paragraph dialog box or by selecting an option from the Line Spacing list in the Paragraph group on the Home tab. When you select a line-spacing option, Word calculates the spacing based on the largest font size in the line. For example, if the line contains all 12-point text except for one word in 24-point text, line spacing set at Double will be 48 pt rather than 24 pt. Thus, if there is more than one font size in a paragraph, you might want to use the "Exactly" setting to set line spacing.

The following table lists the six line-spacing options in the Paragraph dialog box.

Option	Description
Single	Sets the line spacing to one line, or 1.0.
1.5 lines	Sets the line spacing to one-and-a-half lines.
Double	Sets the line spacing to two lines, or 2.0.
At least	Sets a minimum amount of space between lines. It's measured in points, which you specify.
Exactly	Sets an exact line spacing, measured in points, which you specify, and does not adjust the spacing to accommodate changes in font size.
Multiple	Sets the line spacing to accommodate multiple lines. The default for this setting is three lines.

Do it!

D-4: Setting line spacing for a paragraph

Here's how	Here's why
1 Place the insertion point in the first paragraph on page 1	
2 Drag to the bottom of the page	To select the paragraphs.
3 Activate the Home tab	
In the Paragraph group, click	(The Line Spacing button.) To display the Line Spacing menu.
Choose **1.5**	To set the line spacing to 1.5 lines.
4 Deselect the text	You've increased the space between the lines.
5 Update and close all open documents	

Topic E: Automatic formatting

This topic covers the following Microsoft Certified Application Specialist exam objective for Word 2007.

#	Objective
2.1.4	**Format paragraphs** • Format quoted material

The AutoFormat feature

Explanation

The AutoFormat feature applies formatting to various items—such as headings, bulleted and numbered lists, quotation marks, and fractions—as you type. AutoFormat settings are located on the AutoFormat tab of the AutoCorrect dialog box, shown in Exhibit 4-5. For example, one of the AutoFormat options replaces straight quotes (") with smart quotes (" or ")—also called curly quotes—as you type.

To manage AutoFormat options:

1. Click the Office button and click Word Options to open the Word Options dialog box.
2. In the left pane, select Proofing.
3. Click AutoCorrect Options to open the AutoCorrect dialog box
4. Activate the AutoFormat tab.
5. Check the options that you want to use, and clear the options that you don't want automatically applied as you type.
6. Click OK to close the AutoCorrect dialog box.
7. Click OK to close the Word Options dialog box.

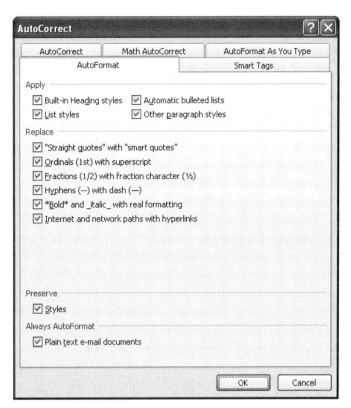

Exhibit 4-8: The AutoFormat options

Do it! **E-1: Using AutoFormat to format quoted text**

Here's how	Here's why
1 Go to the My PR letter document	If necessary.
2 Click [icon]	
Click **Word Options**	To open the Word Options dialog box.
3 In the left pane, select **Proofing**	
Click **AutoCorrect Options**	To open the AutoCorrect Options dialog box.
4 Activate the AutoFormat tab	(Click the tab.) To examine the AutoFormat options.
Observe the option shown	☑ "Straight quotes" with "smart quotes"
	This option is checked by default, indicating that when you type a quotation mark, it will be automatically formatted as a "smart quote."
5 Click **Cancel**	To close the AutoCorrect dialog box.
Click **Cancel**	To close the Word Options dialog box.
6 Place the insertion point to the left of the O in Outlander, as shown	of |Outlander Cooking!
	Located in the first sentence.
Type **"**	To add a quotation mark. Notice that it's automatically changed to a smart quote.
7 Place the insertion point to the right of the exclamation point (!) and type **"**	Cooking!"
	To add another quotation mark. Word changes the straight quote to a closing smart quote.
8 Update and close the document	

Unit summary: Formatting text

Topic A In this topic, you applied **character formatting** to text. To apply formats, you used the Font dialog box, the Font group, the Mini toolbar, the Repeat command, and the Format Painter.

Topic B In this topic, you used **tabs** to align text. Using the ruler, you set tabs, moved tabs, and cleared tabs. You also used the Tabs dialog box to set a tab with a leader.

Topic C In this topic, you learned about basic **paragraph formatting**, such as changing paragraph alignment. You applied borders and shading. You also used bulleted and numbered lists.

Topic D In this topic, you applied advanced paragraph formatting. You set left and right **indents** and learned about **hanging indents**. You also used **paragraph spacing** to control the amount of space before and after a paragraph. Finally, you learned how to change the **line spacing** in a paragraph.

Topic E In this topic, you examined **AutoFormat** options and used one of these options to replace straight quotes with smart quotes.

Independent practice activity

In this activity, you will apply various formats to text and paragraphs. You'll also set tab stops and adjust paragraph spacing.

1. Open Practice formatting, from the current unit folder, and save it as **My practice formatting**.
2. Format the entire document as Times New Roman.
3. Format the heading, "Thoughts from the President," as bold, 14 pt, and make the font color Accent 2.
4. Format the heading as small caps, and expand the character spacing by 2 pt. (*Hint*: Use the Font dialog box.)
5. Format the first customer comment as italic, 14 pt.
6. Set the left indent for the first customer comment to 1".
7. Use the Format Painter to apply this formatting to the second customer comment.
8. Below the first customer comment, in the line with the customer's name, add a left tab stop at 3.5".
9. For the second customer's name, add a left tab stop at 3.5".
10. Set the space after each paragraph in the document to 12 pt.
11. Update and close the document.

Review questions

1 What are some ways to apply character formats?

2 What technique should you use to apply the same highlighting multiple times?

3 Name the five types of tabs.

4 How do you change the tab type?

5 Which paragraph alignment avoids ragged edges?

6 How do you apply a border around a paragraph?

7 How do you change the format of the bullets in a list without changing the list text?

8 Which of the following describes the left indent marker?

   A The up-pointing triangle at the right side of the ruler

   B The box under the hanging-indent triangle

   C The up-pointing triangle on the left side of the ruler

   D The down-pointing triangle on the left side of the ruler

Unit 5
Tables

Unit time: 45 minutes

Complete this unit, and you'll know how to:

A Create tables and convert text to tables.

B Navigate, select elements, add text, and apply formatting in a table.

C Add and delete rows and columns, change column width, align tables, and convert tables to text.

Topic A: Creating tables

This topic covers the following Microsoft Certified Application Specialist exam objective for Word 2007.

#	Objective
4.2.1	**Create tables and lists** (This objective is also covered in the unit titled "Formatting text.") • Convert text to tables

Using tables to organize content

Explanation

A *table* is made up of rows and columns and is an excellent way to present certain kinds of information. Although you can use tabs to manipulate text so that it appears to be in a table, this process can be time-consuming. When you have a lot of text to align into rows and columns, tables are easier to use. You can create tables in several ways, including creating them from scratch and converting text into a table.

When you create or work with tables, Word adds a set of Table Tools to the Ribbon. These tools consist of two additional Ribbon tabs: Design and Layout.

Creating tables from scratch

To insert a table quickly:

1. Place the insertion point where you want the table to go.
2. Activate the Insert tab.
3. In the Tables group, click the Table button to display the Table gallery, shown in Exhibit 5-1.
4. Point to the squares in the gallery to indicate the size of the table you want to create. As you point, the squares are highlighted, and Word shows a preview of the table in the document.
5. Click the gallery to insert the table.

When creating a table, you specify the number of rows and columns. The intersection of a row and a column is called a *cell*.

Using the Insert Table dialog box

In the Tables group, click Table and choose Insert Table to open the Insert Table dialog box. Here, you can specify the number of columns and rows the new table should have, as well as AutoFit settings.

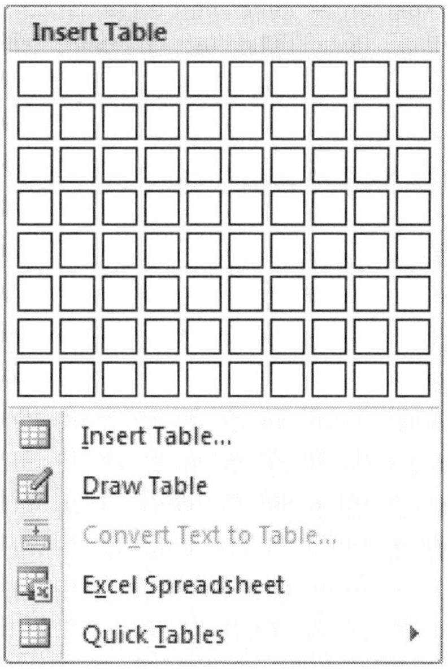

Exhibit 5-1: The Table gallery

Do it!

A-1: Creating a table

Here's how	Here's why
1 Open Tables	From the current unit folder.
Save the document as **My tables**	In the current unit folder.
2 Show nonprinting characters	If necessary.
3 Move to the end of the document	Press Ctrl+End.
4 Activate the Insert tab	
In the Tables group, click **Table**	To display the Table gallery.
Point to the gallery	As you point to the Table gallery, Word highlights squares, which represent table cells. In addition, Word begins to draw the table at the insertion point.
Click as shown	[3x2 Table gallery illustration] To create a table with two rows and three columns.
5 Observe the Ribbon	Word activates the Table Tools, which consist of a Design tab and a Layout tab. These are available only when you're working in tables.

Creating tables from existing text

Explanation

You can convert existing text into a table, which is faster than retyping or copying text into a new table. The text that you want to convert to a table needs to have separator characters to indicate where new columns should begin. Common separator characters are tabs and commas. By default, paragraph marks indicate a new row. If the text doesn't contain separator characters, you should insert them before you proceed.

To convert text to a table:

1. Select the text you want to convert, including the paragraph marks. Make sure the text has separators, such as tab characters, indicating where new columns should start.
2. On the Insert tab, in the Tables group, click Table and choose Convert Text to Table.
3. In the Convert Text to Table dialog box, shown in Exhibit 5-2, Word suggests a number of columns and rows based on the separator characters.
4. If necessary, edit the value in the Number of columns box.
5. If desired, select an AutoFit option.
6. If necessary, select a different column separator under Separate text at.
7. Click OK.

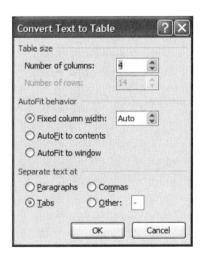

Exhibit 5-2: The Convert Text to Table dialog box

Do it!

A-2: Converting text to a table

Here's how	Here's why
1 Select the indicated text	You'll convert it to a table.

State → City	Store Location	Projected Revenues (in $ thousands)¶
MD → Baltimore →	Prestige Market →	112¶
MD → Bethesda →	Prestige Market →	175¶
MD → Rockville →	Mediterranean Gourmet →	80¶
NJ → Cherry Hill →	Patterson's Grocers →	180¶
NJ → Trenton →	Roma →	75¶
NY → Albany →	Prestige Market →	95¶
NY → Buffalo →	Mediterranean Gourmet →	60¶
NY → New York →	Patterson's Grocers →	215¶
NY → New York →	Village Gourmet Bakery →	230¶
PA → Harrisburg →	Patterson's Grocers →	140¶
PA → Philadelphia →	Patterson's Grocers →	165¶
VA → Charlottesville →	Roma →	120¶
VA → Fairfax →	Mediterranean Gourmet →	110¶

Here's how	Here's why
2 Activate the Insert tab	If necessary.
Display the Table gallery	In the Tables group, click Table.
Choose **Convert Text to Table...**	To open the Convert Text to Table dialog box.
3 Under Separate text at, verify that Tabs is selected	Word will base the number of columns on the location of tabs in the selected text.
Click **OK**	To create the table from the selected text.
4 Deselect the text	
5 Update the document	

Topic B: Working with table content

Explanation

You can move within a table by using the keyboard or the mouse. You can also select the various table elements, and apply character and paragraph formatting to the text in a table.

Moving within a table

To use the mouse to move in a table, click in a cell to place the insertion point. The following table lists the options for using the keyboard to move in a table:

Press this	To move
Tab	One cell to the right.
Shift+Tab	One cell to the left.
Up Arrow	Up one row.
Down Arrow	Down one row.
Alt+Home	To the first cell in the row.
Alt+End	To the last cell in the row.
Alt+Page Up	To the first cell in the column.
Alt+Page Down	To the last cell in the column.

Do it!

B-1: Navigating in a table

Here's how	Here's why
1 Place the insertion point in the first cell of the top row	The cell with "State" in it.
2 Press TAB	To move one cell to the right.
3 Press TAB again	To move one more cell to the right.
4 Press ↓ twice	To move down two rows.
5 Press ↑	To move up one row.
6 Press SHIFT + TAB	To move one cell to the left.
7 Using the keyboard, move the insertion point back to the first cell	

Selecting parts of a table

Explanation

Sometimes you'll need to select various parts of a table. For example, you might want to apply a border to a cell or row. To do this, you need to select the table element, as opposed to selecting only the text in it. When you select a table element, it's highlighted.

The following table lists techniques for using the mouse to select table elements:

Element	Selection technique
Table	Click the table-move handle that appears in the upper-left region of the table when you point to the table. You must be in Print Layout or Web Layout view to see the table-move handle.
Column	Point just inside the top border of a column until the mouse pointer becomes a small, black arrow that points down. Then click.
Row	In the selection bar, point to the row, and then click. Or point to the left edge of any cell in the row; when the pointer becomes an arrow, double-click.
Cell	Point just inside the left border of the cell until the mouse pointer becomes a small, black arrow that points to the right; then click. You can also triple-click inside the cell.

In addition to these techniques, you can use the Select button in the Table group on the Layout tab. Place the insertion point in the table, click Select, and choose an option from the drop-down menu.

Do it!

B-2: Selecting table elements

Here's how	Here's why
1 Triple-click the indicated cell	To select it.
2 Place the insertion point in the second cell of the second row	The row containing "Baltimore."
Drag as shown	To select multiple cells.
3 In the selection bar, point to the first row of the table and click	To select the row.
4 Point to the indicated area	
	The pointer changes to a downward-pointing arrow.
Click the mouse	To select the City column
5 Click as shown	
	Clicking the table-move handle selects the entire table.
6 Deselect the table	Click in the document area outside the table.

Adding text to a table

Explanation

After you've created a table, you're ready to add text or numbers to it. To do so:

1. Place the insertion point in the desired cell.
2. Type the text or numbers.
3. Press Tab to move one cell to the right.
4. When you come to the end of a row, press Tab to move to the first cell of the next row. If no row exists, Word will insert one automatically, and it will inherit the formatting of the previous row. If you press Enter after typing, you'll create a new paragraph in the same cell.

Do it!

B-3: Entering text in a table

Here's how	Here's why
1 In the bottom table, place the insertion point in the first cell of the top row	
2 Type **Total States**	
3 Press TAB	To move to the next cell.
Type **Total Cities**	
4 Move to the next cell	Press Tab.
Type **Total Locations**	
5 Complete the table as shown	

Total·States¤	Total·Cities¤	Total·Locations¤
5¤	14¤	15¤

6 Update the document

Character and paragraph formatting in tables

Explanation

You might want to draw the reader's attention to a specific value in a cell. You can do this by applying character and paragraph formats. To apply character and paragraph formatting to text in a table, use the same techniques that you would use to format text in a document. There are also some formatting options available only for tables. For example, to align the contents of a cell, use the commands in the Alignment group on the Layout tab.

Do it!

B-4: Formatting text in a table

Here's how	Here's why
1 Select the first row of the top table	(In the selection bar, point to the row and click.) Because the first row contains headings, you'll format them to differentiate them from the other data.
2 Change the font to Arial	If necessary, activate the Home tab.
Format the text as bold	
Deselect the text	
3 Select the first column	Point to the top of the column until the pointer changes to a downward-pointing arrow, and click.
4 Under Table Tools, activate the Layout tab	
5 In the Alignment group, click as shown	(The Align Center button.) To center the contents of the selected cells vertically as well as horizontally.
6 Center the text in the first row	Select the row and apply the formatting.
7 Format the first row of the second table as Arial, bold	You might need to activate the Home tab.
8 Update the document	

Topic C: Changing table structure

This topic covers the following Microsoft Certified Application Specialist exam objectives for Word 2007.

#	Objective
4.2.1	Create tables and lists • Convert tables to text
4.3.2	Modify table properties and options • Insert and delete rows and columns

Options for modifying tables

Explanation

As you work with a table, you might need to modify it by inserting rows or columns. When you insert a column, Word might automatically adjust the width of all the columns to keep the table within the page margins; this depends on whether the table fills the space between the margins. You might also want to delete rows or columns, change column widths, or even delete an entire table. You can also convert a table to regular text.

Adding rows and columns

You can add rows and columns to a table by using the options in the Rows & Columns group on the Layout tab. You can also right-click the table and use the shortcut menu. The following table lists techniques for adding rows and columns.

To add...	Do this
A row to the bottom of a table	Place the insertion point in the last cell of the last row, and press Tab.
A row to the middle of a table	Place the insertion point in an existing row. In the Rows & Columns group, click Insert Above or Insert Below; or right-click and choose Insert, Insert Rows Above or Insert Rows Below.
Multiple rows in the middle of a table	Select as many rows as you want to insert. In the Rows & Columns group, click Insert Above or Insert Below; or right-click and choose Insert, Insert Rows Above or Insert Rows Below.
A column	Place the insertion point in a column. In the Rows & Columns group, click Insert Right or Insert Left; or right-click and choose Insert, Insert Columns to the Left or Insert Columns to the Right.
Multiple columns in the middle of a table	Select as many columns as you want to add. In the Rows & Columns group, click Insert Right or Insert Left; or right-click and choose Insert, Insert Columns to the Left or Insert Columns to the Right.

Tables **5–13**

Do it!

C-1: Adding rows and columns

Here's how	Here's why
1 In the top table, place the insertion point in the last cell of the bottom row	The cell containing "110."
2 Press `TAB`	To add a new row.
3 Press `TAB` four more times	To create a second new row.
4 In the first new row, type the indicated text	

| VA¤ | Richmond¤ | Prestige·Market¤ | 85¤ |

5 In the top table, place the insertion point in any cell in the fifth row	The row contains information for the Patterson's Grocers location in Cherry Hill, NJ.
Activate the Layout tab	Under Table Tools, on the Ribbon.
In the Rows & Columns group, click **Insert Above**	To insert a row above the current one.
In the new row, type the indicated text	

| NJ¤ | Atlantic·City¤ | Roma¤ | 136¤ |

6 In the bottom table, select the third column	Point to the top of the third column ("Total Locations") until the pointer changes to a downward-pointing arrow, and then click.
In the Rows & Columns group, click **Insert Right**	To insert a column to the right of the current one.
In the new column, type the indicated text	Total·Projected·Revenue¤ $1,978,000¤
7 Update the document	

Deleting columns, rows, and tables

Explanation

You can delete rows and columns from tables, or delete an entire table, by using commands in the Rows & Columns group or by pressing Backspace. However, you can't delete rows, columns, or tables by pressing Delete. The Delete key deletes only the text in a table, not the table structure itself.

Do it!

C-2: Deleting columns, rows, and an entire table

Here's how	Here's why
1 Select the first column of the top table	
Press DELETE	You've cleared the text from the column, but the column itself remains.
Undo the deletion	Press Ctrl+Z.
2 On the Layout tab, in the Table group, click **Select**	To display a drop-down menu.
Choose **Select Table**	To select the entire table.
Press ← BACKSPACE	To delete the entire table.
Undo the deletion	
3 Select the bottom row of the top table	The empty row.
Right-click the row	To display the shortcut menu.
Choose **Delete Rows**	To delete the row.
4 Update the document	

Changing column width

Explanation

You can manually change the width of table columns by using the Table Properties dialog box, by dragging the column boundaries, or by using the options in the Cell Size group (on the Layout tab). In the Cell Size group, you can also use the AutoFit commands to automatically change the width of columns to fit the text in the cells or to have the table fill the page width.

Do it!

C-3: Changing the width of a column

Here's how	Here's why
1 Observe the Store Location column in the top table	Some store locations wrap to a second line. You'll increase the width of the column.
2 Select the Store Location column	
3 On the Layout tab, in the Cell Size group, click as shown	
	(The up-arrow in the Table Column Width box). To increase the cell width. The location names now fit on a single line, reducing the overall height of the table.
4 Place the insertion point in the bottom table	
5 In the Cell Size group, click **AutoFit**	
Choose **AutoFit Contents**	To automatically resize the width of each column to fit its contents.
6 Point to the indicated area	
	The right boundary of the rightmost column in the bottom table.
Press and hold the mouse on the column boundary	To display a dotted line, indicating the position of the boundary on the horizontal ruler.
Drag to the left	To move the boundary and change the column's width.
Drag the boundary to the **5"** mark	
7 Place the insertion point in the table	If necessary.
In the Cell Size group, click	(The Distribute Columns button.) To distribute the columns evenly.
8 Update the document	

Aligning tables

Explanation

You can change how a table is aligned within the document margins by using the Alignment options on the Table tab of the Table Properties dialog box, shown in Exhibit 5-3. To open this dialog box, right-click a table and choose Table Properties. The alignment options are:

- **Left** — The table is aligned with the left margin.
- **Center** — The table is centered between the left and right margins.
- **Right** — The table is aligned with the right margin.

Note, however, that this is different from aligning text within the table. Text alignment controls are located in the Alignment group on the Layout tab (under Table Tools on the Ribbon).

Exhibit 5-3: The Table Properties dialog box

Do it!

C-4: Aligning a table

Here's how	Here's why
1 Place the insertion point in the bottom table	If necessary.
2 Right-click and choose **Table Properties...**	To open the Table Properties dialog box, shown in Exhibit 5-3.
3 Verify that the Table tab is active	
4 Under Alignment, click **Center**	To center the table relative to the page margins.
Click **OK**	To close the dialog box.
5 Update the document	

Converting tables to text

Explanation

You can transform a table of information into regular text by using the Convert Table to Text dialog box, shown in Exhibit 5-4. To change a table into text:

1 Place the insertion point in the table you want to convert.
2 On the Layout tab, in the Data group, click Convert to Text.
3 In the Convert Table to Text dialog box, specify how you'd like the text to be separated after the conversion.
4 Click OK.

Exhibit 5-4: The Convert Table to Text dialog box

Do it!

C-5: Converting a table to text

Here's how	Here's why
1 Verify that the insertion point is in the bottom table	
2 On the Layout tab, in the Data group, click **Convert to Text**	To open the Convert Table to Text dialog box.
3 Verify that Tabs is selected	To use a tab character to separate the contents of each table cell in a row.
4 Click **OK**	To convert the table to text.
Deselect the text	
5 Update and close the document	

Unit summary: Tables

Topic A   In this topic, you learned that **tables** provide a structured way to present information, and you created a table. You also **converted text to a table**.

Topic B   In this topic, you **navigated** in a table by using the keyboard. You also **selected** table elements. Then you added text in a table and applied character and paragraph **formatting** to the text.

Topic C   In this topic, you modified tables by **adding rows** and **columns** and by deleting rows, columns, and tables. You also **changed column widths**. Finally, you **aligned** a table on the page.

Independent practice activity

In this activity, you'll create a document and insert a table. Then you'll insert text in the table and format it.

1 Create a new, blank document, and save it as **My practice tables** in the current unit folder.

2 Insert a table with four columns and four rows.

3 Add the text in the first four rows, as shown in Exhibit 5-5. (You'll format the text later.)

4 Add a fifth row to the table.

5 Add the text in the fifth row, as shown in Exhibit 5-5. (The text in the final cell might wrap to a second line in the cell.)

6 Select the first row.

7 Format the font as 14 pt, bold.

8 Center the text in the first row.

9 Change the width of the last column to fit all of the text on one line. (*Hint:* Select the last column and use the AutoFit Contents command; then select the entire table and use the AutoFit Window command.)

10 Compare your table to Exhibit 5-5.

11 Update and close the document.

Tea	Vendor	Order status	Comments
Oolong	East Seas	En route	2 weeks late
Darjeeling	China Clipper	In warehouse	Excellent product
Earl Grey	House of Lords	In warehouse	Not fresh
House blend	China Clipper	Shipping next week	New product from this vendor

Exhibit 5-5: The document after Step 10 of the independent practice activity

Review questions

1 Why is it better to create a table, instead of using tabs to simulate the appearance of a table?

2 When you convert existing text into a table, how is the text divided into rows and columns?

3 How can you insert multiple columns in the middle of a table?

4 What happens when you use the Delete key in a table?

5 You've selected a row that you want to delete from a table. Which key should you press?

6 Which command automatically resizes the width of each table column to fit its contents?

Unit 6
Page layout

Unit time: 30 minutes

Complete this unit, and you'll know how to:

A Add headers and footers to a document.

B Set and change the margins of a document, change page orientation, and set text-flow options.

C Add and delete manual page breaks.

Topic A: Headers and footers

This topic covers the following Microsoft Certified Application Specialist exam objectives for Word 2007.

#	Objective
1.2.1	**Format pages** • Page numbers
1.2.2	**Create and modify headers and footers (Not using Quick Parts)** • Create different first pages • Add or modify page numbers in headers and footers (This objective is also covered in *Word 2007: Intermediate*, in the unit titled "Sections and columns.")

Adding headers and footers to a document

Explanation

A *header* is text that appears at the top of a page, in the margin area, as shown in Exhibit 6-1. A *footer* is text that appears in the bottom margin. When you're working in the main document area, the header and footer areas are dimmed, indicating that they aren't available for editing. To enter or edit text in a header or footer, you first have to activate the header or footer area. If a header or footer already exists, do this by double-clicking the header and footer area. Otherwise, use the commands in the Header & Footer group on the Insert tab to activate and edit these areas.

Headers and footers are visible only in Print Layout view. Even if the header and footer text isn't shown on screen, it will appear in the printed document.

To create a header:

1. Activate the Insert tab.
2. In the Header & Footer group, click Header to display the Header gallery.
3. Select a header from the gallery, or chose Edit Header to create an unformatted header.

The procedure for creating a footer is similar, except that you would click Footer in the Header & Footer group.

When you create or work with headers and footers, Word displays the Header & Footer Tools. These are on a Design tab added to the Ribbon.

Exhibit 6-1: An example of a header

Do it!

A-1: Creating a header and footer

Here's how	Here's why
1 Open Cookbook	(From the current unit folder.) You'll add a header and footer to the document.
Save the document as **My cookbook**	In the current unit folder.
2 Display nonprinting characters	If necessary.
3 Activate the Insert tab	
4 In the Header & Footer group, click **Header**	To display the Header gallery.
Choose **Alphabet**	Title A·word·from·the·chairman¶ To apply the Alphabet header style. Word automatically inserts a title into the header, based on the text in your document.
Observe the Ribbon	The Header & Footer Tools have appeared, and there is now a Design tab on the Ribbon.
5 Click **Footer** and choose **Alphabet**	(In the Header & Footer group.) To apply this footer style to the document. This style includes the page number, which Word updates automatically.
6 In the Navigation group, click **Go To Header**	To activate the header area.
7 In the Close group, click **Close Header and Footer**	To return to the main document area. The Header & Footer Tools disappear from the Ribbon.
8 Update the document	

Editing text in headers and footers

Explanation

You can edit the text in headers and footers by using the same editing techniques you use in the document area. You can also delete headers and footers. To edit the text in a header or footer, first double-click the header or footer to activate it, and then modify the text as needed. You can also activate the header or footer by using the commands in the Header & Footer group, on the Insert tab. To do so, in the Header & Footer group, click either Header or Footer and choose Edit Header or Edit Footer.

Different headers and footers for different pages

You might want the first page of a document to have a header and footer that are different from those that appear in the rest of the document. To create a unique first-page header and footer, first make sure the Headers & Footer Tools are active. Then, in the Options group on the Design tab, check Different First Page. Edit or format the first-page header and footer as necessary.

You can also create different headers and footers for odd and even pages by checking Different Odd & Even Pages. The header areas are labeled in the document as "Even Page Header" and "Odd Page Header," and the footer areas are labeled similarly.

Do it!

A-2: Editing headers and footers

Here's how	Here's why
1 Double-click the header area	(You might need to scroll up to view the header area.) To activate it.
Drag to select the current title	*Title* A·word·from·the·chairman¶
2 Type **Outlander Cooking!**	
Format the text as Trebuchet MS, italic	Click the Italic button in the Font group on the Home tab.
3 Scroll down to the footer	The footer contains the page number. You'll edit the footer so that it contains the words "Spice up your life!" Later, you'll add the page number in the margin.
Click **Type text**	[Type·text]
	To select this area of the footer.
Type **Spice up your life!**	
Format the text as Trebuchet MS, italic	
4 Activate the Header & Footer Tools tab	To make the Design tab available.
In the Options group, check **Different First Page**	To remove the header and footer from the first page. You can designate a header and footer on the first page that are unlike those on the rest of the document pages.
5 Double-click in the document	To deactivate the header and footer areas.
Scroll through the document	To examine the headers and footers.
6 Update the document	

Page numbering

Explanation

Although the Headers & Footer Tools tab can be used to add page numbers to a document, Word provides more page numbering options. In the Header & Footer group on the Insert tab, click Page Number and choose Top of Page, Bottom of Page, or Page Margins to see these formats and to insert the page number in a document.

Do it!

A-3: Inserting page numbers

Here's how	Here's why
1 Go to the first page	Press Ctrl+Home, if necessary.
Activate the Insert tab	
2 In the Header & Footer group, click **Page Number**	To display the Page Number menu.
Choose **Bottom of Page**, **Plain Number 2**	To insert the page number in the center of the bottom margin for the first page.
3 Scroll to the bottom of the first page	(If necessary.) To view the page number.
Scroll through the document	The page number on the first page is different from the other pages because the Different First Page option is selected.

Page layout **6–7**

Topic B: Margins

This topic covers the following Microsoft Certified Application Specialist exam objective for Word 2007.

#	Objective
1.2.1	**Format pages** • Orientation • Margins

Setting margins

Explanation

Margins define the amount of space between the document content and the top, bottom, left, and right edges of a page. By default, the top and bottom margins are set at 1", and the left and right margins are set at 1.25". You can set custom margins for a document, but there are some things to keep in mind. First, in general, margins affect all pages in a document. Second, headers and footers are contained in the top and bottom margins, so if you decrease the margins too much, the header and footer information might not print completely.

You can adjust the margins by using the rulers in Print Layout view or by using the Margins tab of the Page Setup dialog box. You can also select a set of margin settings from the Margins gallery. In the Page Setup group (on the Page Layout tab), click Margins, and select an option.

Adjusting margins in Print Layout view

You can change the margins in Print Layout view by dragging the margin boundaries on the ruler. (When you point to a margin boundary, the pointer becomes a two-headed arrow.) You can see the effect on the page immediately.

Print Layout view displays horizontal and vertical rulers. Use the horizontal ruler, shown in Exhibit 6-2, to change the left and right margins. Use the vertical ruler to change the top and bottom margins.

Exhibit 6-2: The left and right margins on the horizontal ruler

Do it!

B-1: Using Print Layout view to adjust margins

Here's how	Here's why
1 Point to the right side of the horizontal ruler as shown	
	(The pointer should change to a horizontal two-headed arrow.) You can change the margins in Print Layout view by dragging their boundaries on the ruler.
Drag the right margin boundary as shown	
	To decrease the margin, thus increasing the space available for the main document content.
2 Decrease the left margin	(Drag the left margin boundary on the horizontal ruler.) Print Layout view is good for "eyeballing" page layout, but you can't set margins precisely.
3 Scroll through the document	You've adjusted the margins for all pages.
4 Update the document	

The Page Setup dialog box

Explanation

You can also change margins by using the Page Setup dialog box. There, you can specify an exact measurement for each margin.

On the Ribbon, activate the Page Layout tab. Then, in the Page Setup group, click the Dialog Box Launcher to open the Page Setup dialog box. (You can also open the Page Setup dialog box by opening the Margins gallery and choosing Custom Margins.) Activate the Margins tab, shown in Exhibit 6-3, and edit the values in the Top, Bottom, Left, and Right boxes.

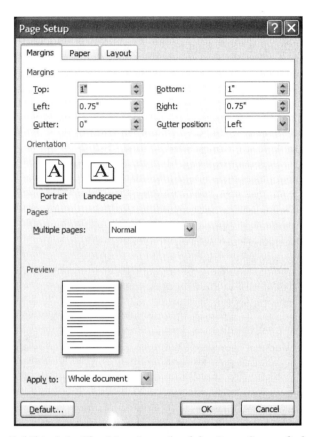

Exhibit 6-3: The Margins tab of the Page Setup dialog box

Page orientation

You can create documents with one of two *page orientations*: landscape orientation makes the page 11"×8.5", and portrait orientation (the default) makes the page 8.5"×11". For certain documents, such as charts, tables, certificates, or mailers, you might choose the landscape orientation. You can change the orientation for an entire document or only certain parts of a document.

To change the orientation of a document:
1. Open the Page Setup dialog box.
2. Activate the Margins tab.
3. Under Orientation, click Portrait or Landscape.
4. From the Apply to list, select an option:
   - Whole document — Applies the new settings to the entire document.
   - This point forward — Applies the new settings to the document, starting at the insertion point and for any subsequent pages.
   - Selected text — If you've selected some text, creates a new section with the new settings.
5. Click OK.

Vertical alignment

You might also want to adjust the vertical alignment of your text. You can align text vertically with the top, center, or bottom of the page, or you can justify the text between the top and bottom margins.

To change the vertical alignment of a document:
1. Open the Page Setup dialog box.
2. Activate the Layout tab.
3. From the Vertical alignment list, select the type of alignment you want to use.
4. Click OK.

Do it!

B-2: Setting margins and page orientation

Here's how	Here's why
1 On the Page Layout tab, in the Page Setup group, click **Margins**	To open the Margins gallery.
Choose **Custom Margins...**	To open the Page Setup dialog box.
2 Observe the dialog box	By entering values, you can make more precise adjustments in the margins. You also can change the page orientation of the page and select options (such as mirror margins) for multiple pages.
3 Edit the Left and Right boxes to read **1.25"**	To set the left and right margins precisely at 1.25" each.
4 Under Orientation, click **Landscape**	To indicate that the document should be wider than it is tall.
Under Preview, in the Apply to list, verify that Whole document is selected	To apply the orientation settings to the entire document.
5 Click **OK**	To close the dialog box. The page orientation changes to landscape.
6 In the Page Setup group, click **Orientation**	
Choose **Portrait**	To return the orientation to portrait.
7 Update the document	

Line and page break options

Explanation

The Line and Page Breaks tab of the Paragraph dialog box, shown in Exhibit 6-4, has various options for controlling text flow. The following table describes some of these options.

Option	Description
Widow/Orphan control	A *widow* is a paragraph's last line printed by itself at the beginning of a page. An *orphan* is a paragraph's first line printed by itself at the bottom of a page. This option prevents widows and orphans and is selected by default.
Keep with next	As you edit a document or change its layout, you might find that a heading and the body-text paragraph after it are on different pages. Check this option to keep the selected paragraph and the one following it on the same page.
Keep lines together	Check this option to ensure that all the lines of a selected paragraph stay on the same page.

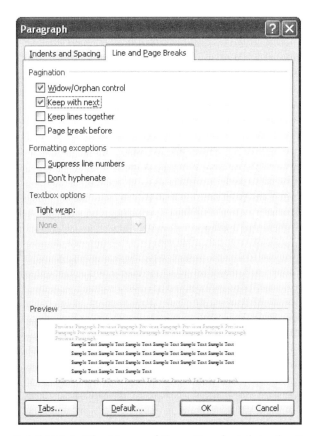

Exhibit 6-4: The Line and Page Breaks tab in the Paragraph dialog box

Do it!

B-3: Applying text-flow options

Here's how	Here's why
1 Move to the bottom of page 3	
Observe the subheading "Spices as modern medicine"	Because of the spacing on this page, the subheading is on one page, and the next body paragraph is on another page. You'll apply text-flow options to keep this heading on the same page as the paragraph to which it's referring.
2 Place the insertion point in the subheading	
3 Open the Paragraph dialog box	On either the Home tab or the Page Layout tab, in the Paragraph group, click the Dialog Box Launcher.
Activate the Line and Page Breaks tab	
4 Under Pagination, observe the settings	Widow/Orphan control is checked by default.
5 Check **Keep with next**	
6 Click **OK**	To close the dialog box. The subheading moves to the next page.
7 Update the document	

Topic C: Page breaks

This topic covers the following Microsoft Certified Application Specialist exam objective for Word 2007.

#	Objective
2.3.1	Insert and delete page breaks

Changing pagination

Explanation

When you have more text than will fit on a page, Word creates a new page, inserting a separator called a *page break*. The process of separating text into pages is called *pagination*. Word automatically inserts page breaks as needed; however, such breaks might not always occur where you want them. If this is the case, you can paginate a document manually by inserting your own page breaks.

Pagination is affected by the margins, the page orientation, and the size and amount of text (or graphics) on a page. Any time you change these attributes, you should check pagination before printing the document.

Automatic vs. manual page breaks

Automatic and manual page breaks are shown differently in the document window. An *automatic page break*—one that Word inserts when the amount of text exceeds the vertical margins—appears either as a solid black line or as space between pages in Print Layout view. (This depends on whether you have white space showing.) *Manual page breaks*—those you insert yourself—appear as closely spaced dotted lines with the words "Page Break" inserted in the middle. Manual-page-break lines are visible only if you're displaying nonprinting characters.

Adding a manual page break

To insert a manual page break:

1. Place the insertion point directly to the left of the text that you want on a new page.
2. Press Ctrl+Enter, or, on the Insert tab, in the Pages group, click Page Break.

To delete a manual page break, select it and press Delete. Although you can't delete an automatic page break, you can insert a manual page break before it to change the pagination.

Do it!

C-1: Adding and deleting manual page breaks

Here's how	Here's why
1 Show nonprinting characters	If necessary.
2 Move to the bottom of page 1	
Observe the bottom of the page	Notice the dotted line with the words "Page Break" in the center. This is a manual page break.
3 Move to page 3	
4 Place the insertion point as shown	*The medicinal use of spices*¶ ¶ *Spices as ancient medicine*¶
	You'll insert a page break at this point.
5 Activate the Insert tab	
In the Pages group, click **Page Break**	To insert a manual page break. The subheading now appears at the top of page 4, but you want to break the page at the subheading above this one.
6 Move to page 3	
7 Click the page break	To place the insertion point.
Press DELETE	To delete the page break.
8 Place the insertion point as shown	¶ *The medicinal use of spices*¶ ¶ *Spices as ancient medicine*¶
9 Press CTRL + ↵ ENTER	To insert a page break.
10 Insert a page break immediately before the subheading "The spice trade"	(Near the bottom of page 4.) To move the subheading "The spice trade" to the top of the next page.
11 Update and close the document	

Unit summary: Page layout

Topic A In this topic, you learned that **headers** and **footers** can be used to add information such as dates and page numbers to documents. Then you created headers and footers and edited them. Finally, you inserted **page numbers**.

Topic B In this topic, you controlled how close your text is to the edge of the page by setting **margins**. You set margins by dragging their boundaries on the ruler in Print Layout view and then by using the Page Setup dialog box. You also kept paragraphs together by using **text-flow options**, such as Widow/Orphan control and Keep with next.

Topic C In this topic, you forced text to begin on a new page by inserting **page breaks**. You also deleted page breaks.

Independent practice activity

In this activity, you'll insert a header and footer. Then you'll adjust the margins.

1. Open Practice layout, from the current unit folder, and save it as **My practice layout**.
2. Insert the header with the Stacks style. (*Hint:* You might need to scroll the list of header options.)
3. Insert the Pinstripes footer. (*Hint:* You might need to scroll the list of footer options.)
4. In the footer, change "Type text" to your name.
5. Change the left and right margins to 1.75". (*Hint*: Use the Page Setup dialog box.)
6. Update and close the document.

Review questions

1 What are the two ways to open the header and footer area?

2 How do you return to the main document area after you're done working in a header or footer?

3 What are the default top, bottom, left, and right margin settings?

4 Which view enables you to adjust the page margins by dragging the margin boundaries?

5 Which dialog box is used to control widows and orphans?

   A Page Setup

   B Paragraph

   C Print Layout

   D Page Break

6 True or false? You can delete an automatic page break.

Unit 7
Proofing and printing documents

Unit time: 90 minutes

Complete this unit, and you'll know how to:

A Proof a document and use the thesaurus.

B Use AutoCorrect to insert text automatically.

C Find and replace text by using the Find and Replace dialog box.

D Preview and print documents.

Topic A: Checking spelling and grammar

This topic covers the following Microsoft Certified Application Specialist exam objective for Word 2007.

#	Objective
1.4.2	Change research options

Using proofing tools

Explanation

You can use the Spelling and Grammar dialog box to check the spelling in a document. You can correct misspellings, add words to the dictionary, and instruct Word to ignore certain spellings that it flags as possibly incorrect. You can open the Spelling and Grammar dialog box by pressing F7 or by clicking Spelling & Grammar in the Proofing group on the Review tab.

To check the spelling of a document manually:

1. Move to the beginning of the document.
2. Open the Spelling and Grammar dialog box, shown in Exhibit 7-1.
3. When the dialog box shows a word that might be misspelled, do any of the following:

    - If the correct word is listed in the Suggestions box, select it and click Change. If the word is misspelled more than once, you can click Change All to change all occurrences of the word.
    - Click Ignore Once or Ignore All to leave the word spelled the way it is.
    - Click Add to Dictionary to add the word to the dictionary so it will be recognized as correct in future spelling checks.

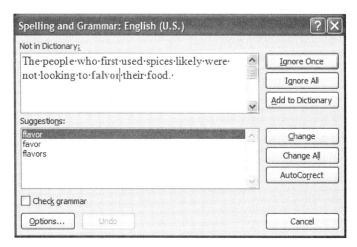

Exhibit 7-1: The Spelling and Grammar dialog box

Changing the default dictionary

The default dictionary is Custom.dic. To change the dictionary that's used during spelling checks:

1 Click the Options button in the Spelling and Grammar dialog box to open the Word Options dialog box with the Proofing section active.
2 Click Custom Dictionaries.
3 Create a new custom dictionary, or add an existing one:
   - To create a custom dictionary, click New and save the dictionary with a name of your choice. Add words to the new dictionary either by selecting it and clicking Edit Word List or by clicking Add to Dictionary in the Spelling and Grammar dialog box.
   - To use an existing custom dictionary, click Add and select the dictionary you want to use.
4 Change the default dictionary by selecting it and clicking Change Default.

Do it!

A-1: Checking spelling

Here's how	Here's why
1 Open **Cookbook**	From the current unit folder.
Save the document as **My cookbook**	In the current unit folder.
2 Activate the Review tab	
In the Proofing group, click **Spelling & Grammar**	To open the Spelling and Grammar dialog box.
3 Observe the dialog box	Punctuation: We're excited to present this edition of *Outlander Cooking!*, revised and expanded for 2006.
	Under Punctuation, Word suggests that the exclamation point followed by a comma might be an error. However, because the exclamation point is part of the book title, you'll leave it as is.
4 Clear **Check grammar**	To tell Word not to check for grammatical errors. A dialog box appears, telling you that Word has finished checking the selection.
Click **Yes**	To check the rest of the document. Word finds the misspelled word "falvor" and suggests several possible spellings.
5 Click **Change**	To use the first spelling that Word suggests. Next, Word finds "FluRid." This is a brand name and is spelled correctly. This time, you'll add it to the dictionary so that Word won't mark it as misspelled in other documents.
6 Click **Add to Dictionary**	To add the word to the default dictionary. Word finds the misspelled word "sererity" and suggests some possibilities.
In the Suggestions box, select **severity**	
Click **Change**	To correct the misspelling. Word finds the misspelled word "chilis." Word suggests "chilies," but you know that "chiles" is also an acceptable spelling. You'll confer with a colleague to see which spelling Outlander Spices uses.
7 Click **Close**	
8 Update the document	

Proofing and printing documents

Checking spelling as you type

Explanation

By default, the Spelling and Grammar feature is set to check the spelling of words as you type. Misspelled words are underlined with a wavy red line. To correct these words:

1 Select the word that is underlined in red.
2 Right-click to display a shortcut menu, and then choose one of the following:

- The correct spelling (if it's listed).
- Ignore All, if you want to leave the word spelled the way it is.
- Add to Dictionary, if you want to add the word to Word's dictionary (so that it won't be identified as misspelled in the future).

Do it!

A-2: Using the automatic spelling checker

Here's how	Here's why
1 On page 5, observe the word "chilis"	The wavy red underline indicates a spelling error. You've determined that Outlander Spices uses the spelling "chilies."
2 Right-click **chilis**	To display the shortcut menu. A list of suggested spellings appears at the top.
Choose **chilies**	To replace the misspelled word.
3 Place the insertion point as shown	defeat so easily. He christened the chilies he ate "peppers," believing
	You'll add a word here.
Type **nievely**	
Press (SPACEBAR)	Word underlines the word with a wavy red line, indicating that the word is misspelled.
4 Right-click **nievely**	To display the shortcut menu.
Choose **naively**	To replace the misspelled word with the correct spelling.
5 Update the document	

Checking grammar

Explanation

In addition to checking the spelling, you can use the Spelling and Grammar feature to check the grammar in a document. By default, this option is on. When using the Spelling and Grammar dialog box to check grammar, you're prompted for each grammatical error it finds, and you can correct the error. There are times, however, when you might choose not to make the suggested change because the phrasing that Word sees as an error is an acceptable style choice. If you don't understand a grammar rule, click the Explain button in the dialog box to display information in Microsoft Office Word Help.

Checking grammar automatically

By default, Word checks grammar automatically as you type, and a wavy green line appears under all possible grammatical errors. You can use either the Spelling and Grammar dialog box or the shortcut menu to check grammar. By clearing Check grammar in the Spelling and Grammar dialog box, you can also tell Word to stop checking grammar.

Do it!

A-3: Checking grammar

Here's how	Here's why
1 Move to the beginning of the document	This time, you'll check for grammatical errors.
2 Press F7	To check the spelling and grammar of the document. A message box appears, telling you that the spelling check is complete. Earlier, you told Word not to check for grammatical errors, so you'll need to recheck the document.
Click **OK**	To close the dialog box.
3 Click	
Click **Word Options**	To open the Word Options dialog box.
4 In the left pane, click **Proofing**	
Check **Check grammar with spelling**	(Under "When correcting spelling and grammar in Word.") To enable grammar checking.
Near the bottom of the dialog box, click **Recheck Document**	A message box appears, stating that words you previously chose to ignore will again appear as misspelled.
Click **Yes**	To close the message box.
Click **OK**	To close the Word Options dialog box.
5 Move to the beginning of the document	Press Ctrl+Home.

Proofing and printing documents **7-7**

6	Press `F7`	This time, Word stops at a possible punctuation error on page 1.
	Click **Explain**	To open Microsoft Office Word Help. The explanation indicates that the punctuation might be unnecessary or misplaced. In this case, it isn't.
	Close Help	
	Click **Ignore Once**	To ignore this instance of the error. However, you still want Word to find other instances of this error, if they occur.
		Word finds a possible capitalization error. However, this time, the suggestion isn't the correct one for this situation.
7	In the Capitalization box, click as shown	valuable·spices·that·he·was·searching·for,·he·did·manage·to·bring·a·previously·unknown·continent·to·the·attention·of·European·explorers·Meanwhile,·however,·Columbus·
		You might need to scroll.
	Type **.**	(Type a period.) The word "Meanwhile" is no longer green; this indicates that there is no longer a grammatical error.
8	Click **Next Sentence**	A message box appears, stating that there are no more spelling or grammar errors.
9	Click **OK**	To close the message box.
10	Update the document	

Using the thesaurus

Explanation

A *thesaurus* provides alternatives, or *synonyms*, for words. You can use Word's thesaurus to find another word with the same or similar meaning to substitute for a word in a document. The thesaurus provides a list of possible substitutions. You can explore these alternatives further by looking up their synonyms as well. Finally, you can also look up an *antonym*, a word with the opposite meaning.

To use the thesaurus:

1. Right-click the word for which you want to find an alternative.
2. In the shortcut menu, point to Synonyms to display a list of synonyms and antonyms.
3. Select the word you want to use.

For more options, display the shortcut menu and choose Synonyms, Thesaurus to open the Research task pane, shown in Exhibit 7-2.

Exhibit 7-2: The thesaurus in the Research task pane

The Research task pane

In addition to the thesaurus, Word contains several research sources you can use to look up information about words. The sources include the Encarta Dictionary and Translation reference books. You also can use the Research task pane to access information online. By default, Word includes North American research sources. To add research sources from other regions, click Research options in the Research task pane; then check the sources you want to use in the Research Options dialog box.

To open the Research task pane, Alt-click anywhere in the document window. In the Search for box, enter the term you want to research, and then press Enter. You can also open the Research task pane by clicking the Research button in the Proofing group.

Do it!

A-4: Finding synonyms and antonyms

Here's how	Here's why
1 Move to page 1	
2 In the first paragraph, right-click **excited**	To display the shortcut menu.
Point to **Synonyms**	To display a list of synonyms and antonyms.
Choose **Thesaurus…**	To open the Research task pane, which displays more choices.
3 Point to **thrilled**, as shown	
Click the down-arrow to the right of "thrilled"	To display a menu with Insert, Copy, and Look Up commands.
Choose **Look Up**	To display meanings and synonyms for the word "thrilled."
Display the commands for the word **delighted**	Point to the word and click the down-arrow to the right of it.
Choose **Insert**	To replace "excited" with "delighted."
4 In the document, select a different word	
Observe the Search for box	Even though the thesaurus is displayed in the task pane, it's still showing the synonyms for "thrilled." You need to activate the thesaurus again.
Press `SHIFT` + `F7`	To activate the thesaurus and search for synonyms for the word you've selected.

5	Click **Research options**	(At the bottom of the Research task pane.) To open the Research Options dialog box.
	Observe the available services	Reference books and other resources are listed. Check the services that you'd like to use. You can also add, remove, or update services.
	Click **Cancel**	To close the Research Options dialog box.
6	Close the Research task pane	
7	Update the document	

Topic B: Using AutoCorrect

This topic covers the following Microsoft Certified Application Specialist exam objective for Word 2007.

#	Objective
1.4.1	Customize Word options • Customize AutoCorrect options

Correcting errors as you type

Explanation

Automated tasks in Word include the AutoCorrect, AutoText, and AutoFormat features. As you type, AutoCorrect corrects common errors, such as commonly misspelled words and incorrect capitalization.

AutoCorrect has a list of default entries that are common typing mistakes. It corrects these mistakes as soon as you press Spacebar, press Enter, or type a punctuation mark. For example, if you type "bcak" instead of "back," AutoCorrect automatically replaces the misspelled word with the correctly spelled word when you press Spacebar.

In addition to correcting commonly misspelled words, AutoCorrect recognizes improper capitalization. For example, if you type "monday," AutoCorrect automatically capitalizes the first letter, changing the word to "Monday."

You can also use AutoCorrect to insert symbols in your documents. The following table shows some of them.

Type this	AutoCorrect replaces with this
(c)	©
(r)	®
(tm)	™

Sometimes, you might not want AutoCorrect to "fix" your spelling or quotation marks. For example, say that you type a quotation mark, which Word turns into a smart quote (" or "), but you want an inch mark ("). In that case, press Crtl+Z to undo the correction, and then continue typing.

Do it!

B-1: Examining AutoCorrect

Here's how	Here's why
1 Open PR letter	From the current unit folder.
Save the document as **My PR letter**	In the current unit folder.

Proofing and printing documents **7-13**

2	Click [icon]	
	Click **Word Options**	To open the Word Options dialog box.
3	In the left pane, click **Proofing**	
	Click **AutoCorrect Options**	To open the AutoCorrect dialog box.
	Verify that the AutoCorrect tab is active	
4	Examine the check boxes	By default, all the options are checked. You can choose which types of corrections AutoCorrect will make.
	Verify that "Replace text as you type" is checked	This option tells AutoCorrect to correct your errors as you type.
5	Observe the Replace and With boxes	You can add your own entries to AutoCorrect by using these boxes.
6	Scroll through the list of AutoCorrect entries	You'll see a list of commonly used symbols and common typing errors.
7	Click **Cancel**	To close the AutoCorrect dialog box.
	Click **Cancel**	To close the Word Options dialog box.
8	Place the insertion point as shown	Outlander Spices¶ To: → employees¶
		At the top of the page, at the end of the first line.
	Type **(TM)**	This is the AutoCorrect entry for the trademark symbol. AutoCorrect changes (TM) into the trademark symbol, ™.
9	Place the insertion point as shown	
	Overview¶ As you know, we've recently finished production on |latest edition of Outlander Cooking! If you haven't yet seen a copy of the finished product, they'll be circulating with all of	
		In the first line of the first paragraph of body text, just before the word "latest." The sentence is missing a "the."
	Type **teh**	You're intentionally misspelling the word "the."
	Press SPACEBAR	AutoCorrect automatically corrects the spelling.
10	Update the document	

The AutoCorrect Options button

Explanation

The AutoCorrect Options button appears near text that has been automatically corrected. When you point to the corrected text, an animated icon resembling a lightning bolt appears below it; after a few seconds, the animation stops, and a blue rectangle remains below the corrected text. When you point to either the animated icon or the blue rectangle, it changes to the AutoCorrect Options button. To undo the corrections made, click the AutoCorrect Options button and choose Undo Automatic Corrections.

You can turn off the default AutoCorrect options by clicking the AutoCorrect Options button and choosing Control AutoCorrect Options. In the AutoCorrect dialog box, clear the options that you don't want corrected.

You can also open the AutoCorrect dialog box to modify the default settings. To do so, open the Word Options dialog box, select the Proofing category, and click AutoCorrect Options.

Proofing and printing documents   **7–15**

Do it!   **B-2: Using the AutoCorrect Options button**

Here's how	Here's why
1 Point as shown	on the latest ished produc
	The animated AutoCorrect symbol appears when you point to text that has been automatically corrected. After a few seconds, the symbol changes to a blue line.
2 Point to the blue line	The blue line changes to the AutoCorrect Options button.
Click	Change back to "teh" Stop Automatically Correcting "teh" Control AutoCorrect Options...
	To display the AutoCorrect Options menu. It shows the options to undo the automatic correction and to stop correcting "teh."
Choose **Change back to "teh"**	The word is replaced by "teh" again.
3 Click the AutoCorrect Options button	Point to the misspelled word again to display the button.
Choose **Redo AutoCorrect**	To correct the word again.
4 Update the document	

Adding an AutoCorrect entry

Explanation

Everyone has the habit of misspelling certain words—sometimes, it's difficult to remember whether a particular word is spelled with one "s" or two, for example. With AutoCorrect, you can enter the misspelling and have Word fix it automatically. You can also create an AutoCorrect entry that replaces an abbreviation with a word or phrase you type frequently. For example, you can create an AutoCorrect entry to replace your initials with your full name.

To add an entry to AutoCorrect:

1 Click the Office button and click Word Options to open the Word Options dialog box.
2 In the left pane, select Proofing.
3 Click AutoCorrect Options to open the AutoCorrect dialog box, shown in Exhibit 7-3.
4 In the Replace box, enter the word or words for the entry you want to create.
5 In the With box, enter the abbreviation, word, or phrase you want to use.
6 Click OK.

Exhibit 7-3: The AutoCorrect dialog box

If a word in your document has been corrected with AutoCorrect, you can easily open the AutoCorrect dialog box. Simply place the insertion point in that word and point to the blue line that appears below it; click the AutoCorrect Options button that appears, and choose Control AutoCorrect Options.

Do it!

B-3: Adding an entry to your AutoCorrect list

Here's how	Here's why
1 Place the insertion point as shown	Outlander·Spices™¶ To: → |employees¶ In the second line of the document.
2 Click the AutoCorrect Options button	Point to a word that has been automatically corrected—in this case, either the "TM" in the first line or the word "the" in the first paragraph.
Choose **Control AutoCorrect Options...**	To open the AutoCorrect dialog box.
3 In the Replace box, enter **os**	The initials of the company Outlander Spices.
Press (TAB)	To move to the With box.
Type **Outlander Spices**	To create an AutoCorrect entry that will replace the letters "os" with the company name.
Click **Add**	To add the entry to the AutoCorrect list.
4 Click **OK**	To save the entry and close the AutoCorrect dialog box.
5 Type **os**	Only the occurrences of "os" as the entire word will be automatically corrected. Word will not change "os" if it appears in the middle of a word.
Press (SPACEBAR)	AutoCorrect replaces the letters with the company name.
6 Update and close the document	

Topic C: Finding and replacing text

This topic covers the following Microsoft Certified Application Specialist exam objectives for Word 2007.

#	Objective
2.1.1	**Apply styles** • Change from one style to another (This objective is also covered in *Word 2007: Intermediate*, in the unit titled "Styles.")
2.2.2	**Find and replace text** • Replace text • Replace all • Search for and highlight specific text
5.1.1	**Move a document quickly using the Find and Go To commands** (This objective is also covered in the unit titled "Navigation and selection techniques.")

Using the Find and Replace command

Explanation

You can use Word's Find and Replace commands to quickly change specific items. By using these commands, you can find and, if you like, replace text; but you can also find and replace such things as page breaks and tab characters. In addition, you can search for specific formatting, regardless of the text to which it has been applied. For example, you might want to search for all bold text in a document and replace the bold format with italics.

To access the Find command, you use the Find and Replace dialog box, shown in Exhibit 7-4. By default, Word searches an entire document, beginning from the insertion point. If the insertion point is at a location other than the beginning of a document, Word searches from that point forward and then goes back to the beginning and continues searching until it reaches the insertion point.

Refining your search

You can refine your search by using additional options in the Find and Replace dialog box. When you search for a word for the first time, these options are hidden. To display them, click More. You can use these options alone or in combination. For example, if you select the "Match case" option and search for "Project," Word will find only those instances of the word that begin with an uppercase "P," including the word "Projects." If you select "Match case" and "Find whole words only" and you search for "project," Word will find each instance of "project" in lowercase, but it will not find "projects" because your search criteria specified only exact matches.

To use the Find command:

1. Open the Find and Replace dialog box.
   - On the Home tab, in the Editing group, click Find.
   - Press Ctrl+F.
2. In the Find what box, enter the text you want to find.

3 Click More and select any search criteria you want to use to refine the search. You can click Less to hide the additional search options and reduce the size of the dialog box, which remains open while the search is being executed. (You can still place the insertion point and type in a document while the Find and Replace dialog box is open.)

4 Click Find Next until you've found what you're looking for.

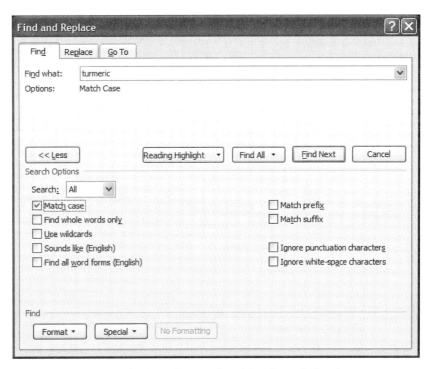

Exhibit 7-4: The Find tab in the Find and Replace dialog box

Do it! **C-1: Searching for a word**

Here's how	Here's why
1 Open Spice info	From the current unit folder.
Save the file as **My spice info**	In the current unit folder.
2 In the Editing group, click **Find**	(On the Home tab.) To open the Find and Replace dialog box.
In the Find what box, enter **bay leaf**	
Click **Find Next**	To search for the first occurrence of "bay leaf." Word found "Bay leaf" in the heading on page 1. (You might need to drag the dialog box out of the way to see the selection.)
3 Click **Find Next**	Word finds the next occurrence of "bay leaf." This time, it's lowercase. You'll tell Word to find only lowercase instances of the text.
4 Click **More**	To display additional search options. The More button changes to Less.
Under Search Options, check **Match case**	
Click **Less**	To hide the additional options again.
5 Click **Find Next**	To find the next occurrence of the phrase in lowercase. Note that in the line just above, "Bay leaf" appears but is capitalized.
Click **Find Next** twice	A message box appears, stating that Word has finished searching the document.
Click **OK**	To close the message box.
6 Click **Cancel**	To close the Find and Replace dialog box.

Replacing text

Explanation

There might be situations when you want to replace several instances of a word or phrase with a different word or phrase. To do this, you can use the Replace command. On the Replace tab of the Find and Replace dialog box, shown in Exhibit 7-5, enter the text you want to replace and the text that you want to use instead.

When you find the first occurrence of the text, you can click the Replace button to replace a single occurrence. Or, to replace all occurrences in one step and bypass further prompts, you can click the Replace All button. Be careful when using this option, though, because you might not want to replace all occurrences of a search term.

To replace text in a document:

1 Open the Find and Replace dialog box.
   - On the Home tab, in the Editing group, click Replace.
   - Press Ctrl+H.
2 In the Find what box, type the text you're replacing.
3 In the Replace with box, type the text you're substituting.
4 Click More if you want to specify additional search options, such as matching case or finding whole words.
5 Click Find Next.
6 Click Replace to replace the text one occurrence at a time, or click Replace All to replace all occurrences at the same time.

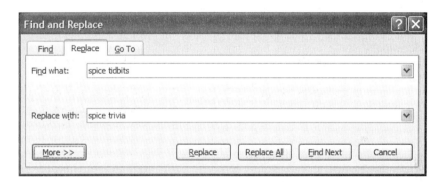

Exhibit 7-5: The Replace tab in the Find and Replace dialog box

Do it!

C-2: Replacing text in a document

Here's how	Here's why
1 In the Editing group, click **Replace**	To open the Find and Replace dialog box with the Replace tab active.
2 Observe the Find what box	
	The text you searched for previously, "bay leaf," appears in the box, and the Match Case option is selected.
3 Edit the Find what box to read **spice tidbits**	You'll change this subheading, which occurs multiple times in the document.
In the Replace with box, enter **spice trivia**	
4 Click **More**	
Clear **Match case**	To find both uppercase and lowercase occurrences.
Click **Less**	
5 Click **Find Next**	To find the first occurrence of the phrase "spice tidbits."
Click **Replace**	Word replaces it with the new phrase, retaining the capitalization of the original. Word then moves to the next occurrence of the search term.
6 Click **Replace All**	A message box appears, stating that Word has made eight replacements.
Click **OK**	To close the message box.
Click **Close**	To close the Find and Replace dialog box.
7 Update and close the document	

Formatting multiple selections

Explanation

When you want to format a document, you can easily select multiple areas at the same time. This saves time because you won't have to repeat your formatting. For example, you might want to format all headings in a similar manner. All you need to do is select a heading, press Ctrl, and select the next heading. After selecting all the headings, you can format them simultaneously.

You can also use the Find feature to simultaneously select text in separate locations and format it. To do so, open the Find and Replace dialog box by pressing Ctrl+F, and leave the Find what and Replace with boxes empty. Click the Format button, as shown in Exhibit 7-6, and choose Font from the menu. Specify the formatting options you want to search for, and then click OK to close the Find Font dialog box. When you click the Find All button, Word finds and highlights all occurrences of the specified format.

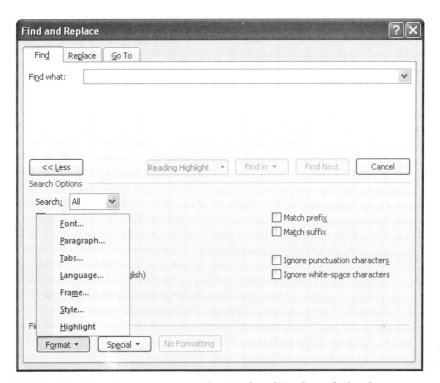

Exhibit 7-6: The Format menu in the Find and Replace dialog box

Do it!

C-3: Formatting multiple selections simultaneously

Here's how	Here's why
1 Switch to the My cookbook document	If necessary.
Move to page 1	A copy editor has added some text to the bottom of page 1. It contains the name of a newsletter, "Outlander Weekly." It's underlined, but you want to change the underlining to italics. You want to quickly find and format all instances of the text.
2 Press CTRL + F	To open the Find and Replace dialog box.
3 In the Find what box, enter **Outlander Weekly**	
4 Click **More**	
Click **Format**	To show the menu of formatting options you can find.
Choose **Font...**	To open the Find Font dialog box.
5 Verify that the Font tab is active	You'll change the underline style.
From the Underline style list, select the indicated option	(On the Font tab.) This is the default underlining style.
Click **OK**	To close the dialog box.

6	Click **Find in**	To display a drop-down menu.
	Choose **Main Document**	To find all occurrences of the specified search term. Word highlights the search terms in the document.
	Click **Close**	To close the Find and Replace dialog box.
7	Press `CTRL` + `I`	To format the selected text as italic.
8	Press `CTRL` + `U`	To remove the underlining from the selected text.
9	Deselect the text	
10	Update the document	

Topic D: Printing documents

This topic covers the following Microsoft Certified Application Specialist exam objective for Word 2007.

#	Objective
1.2.1	Format pages • Paper size

Print options and Print Preview

Explanation

The Print Preview feature helps you see what your document will look like when it's printed. To preview a document, click the Office button and choose Print, Print Preview.

You have several options for printing a document:

- While in Print Preview, click Print to open the Print dialog box.
- Click the Office button and choose Print, Quick Print (or press Ctrl+P) to print one copy of the document with default print settings.

Changing paper size

The default paper size is 8.5"×11"; however, if you're using paper with different dimensions, you can change this default. In Print Preview, in the Page Setup group, you can click the Size button to display a list of other common dimensions. If your paper size is not listed, choose More Paper Sizes to enter custom dimensions.

If you're not in Print Preview, you can change paper size by using the Size button on the Page Layout tab. You can also click the Dialog Box Launcher in the Page Setup group, on the Page Layout tab, to open a dialog box where you can customize paper dimensions.

Do it!

D-1: Previewing a document before printing

Here's how	Here's why
1 Click	
Choose **Print**, **Print Preview**	To display the document in Print Preview.
2 Point to the document page	
	The pointer becomes a magnifying glass with a plus sign in the middle, indicating that clicking will increase the magnification.
Click anywhere in the document	To zoom in to 100% magnification. The pointer becomes a magnifying glass with a minus sign in the middle.
Click the document again	To zoom out so that the entire page fits in the document window.
3 In the Preview group, clear **Magnifier**	
Point to the document	The pointer now appears as it does in Print Layout view, indicating that you can select and edit text.
4 Observe the Page Setup group	While in Print Preview, you can change margin, orientation, and paper size settings.
5 In the Page Setup group, click **Size**	To view other common paper sizes. The default is Letter size, 8.5"×11".
Select **Legal**	To change the paper size to 8.5"×14".
6 Press (PAGE DOWN) several times	To view other pages in the document.
Change the paper size to **Letter**	(In the Page Setup group, click Size and select Letter.) To change the dimensions of the paper size to 8.5"×11".
7 In the Preview group, click **Close Print Preview**	To return to Page Layout view.

The Print dialog box

Explanation

The Print dialog box, shown in Exhibit 7-7, provides a number of options you can set when printing a document. You can change the printer, print specific pages, print multiple copies, collate multiple pages, print even or odd pages, and use Zoom controls to scale and print multiple pages on one sheet of paper.

Under Page range, you can specify which pages you want to print. For example, to print pages 5 to 10, enter "5-10" in the Pages box. You can print multiple copies of a document by specifying a number in the Number of copies box.

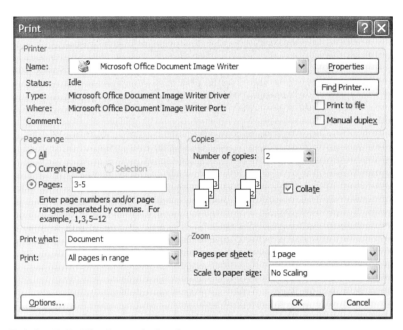

Exhibit 7-7: The Print dialog box

Do it!

D-2: Using the Print dialog box

Here's how	Here's why
1 Click ![icon] Choose **Print**	To open the Print dialog box.
2 Observe the Printer section	You'll see information about the printer to which you're sending the document.
3 Under Page range, in the Pages box, enter **3-5**	To print only pages 3, 4, and 5. (Otherwise, by default, all pages will be printed.) You can also choose to print only the current page or a selection (if you've selected some text).
4 Under Copies, in the Number of copies box, enter **2**	To print two copies. (By default, only one copy is printed and collated.)

Proofing and printing documents **7-29**

5	Display the Print what list	Document **Document** Document properties Document showing markup List of markup Styles AutoText entries Key assignments
		(Click the down-arrow next to the Print what list box.) In addition to printing a document, you can print the document properties, a list of the styles used in the document, and so on.
	Close the list	Click the down-arrow again or press Esc.
6	Display the Print list	(Click the down-arrow next to the Print list box.) You can choose to print all the pages, only the odd pages, or only the even pages of a document.
	Close the list	
7	Click **Options**	To open the Printing section of the Word Options dialog box.
	Observe the dialog box	By default, Word does not update fields or linked data before printing. In addition, by default, hidden text, document properties, and background colors and images are not printed.
	Click **Cancel**	To close the dialog box.
8	Click **OK**	To print the current document. If your computer is not connected to a printer, click Cancel instead.
9	Update and close all documents	

Unit summary: Proofing and printing documents

Topic A In this topic, you located and corrected misspelled words by using the **Spelling and Grammar** dialog box. You also learned how to have Word check spelling automatically as you type. Then you used the grammar checker to check grammar in a document. In addition, you learned how to use the **thesaurus** to find synonyms and antonyms for words.

Topic B In this topic, you learned how Word's **AutoCorrect** feature works. You also added AutoCorrect entries to the AutoCorrect dialog box and used the AutoCorrect Options button.

Topic C In this topic, you searched for text by using the **Find and Replace** dialog box. You also examined search options such as Match Case. You learned how to replace the found text by using the Replace tab in the Find and Replace dialog box.

Topic D In this topic, you used **Print Preview** to preview a document before printing it. Then you learned how to change print settings and print a document by using the **Print** dialog box.

Independent practice activity

In this activity, you'll proof a document for spelling and grammar errors, making decisions about which "errors" to keep and which to change. Then you'll use the thesaurus. Finally, you'll preview and print the document.

1. Open Practice proofing, from the current unit folder, and save it as **My practice proofing**.
2. Correct the spelling and grammar in the document as necessary.
3. Select the word "strive" in the first paragraph on page 1.
4. Use the thesaurus to replace the word "strive" with a word or phrase of your choice.
5. Add an AutoCorrect entry for **Jake O'Connell, President**. Set it so that the name and title are inserted when you type **jo**.
6. Use AutoCorrect to insert the name and title at the bottom of page 1, just before "Outlander Spices." (*Hint*: Press Spacebar after you type **jo**.)
7. Use the Find and Replace dialog box to format all underlined instances of "Outlander Cooking" as italic with no underlining.
8. Preview and print the document. (You don't need to print if you aren't set up to do so.)
9. Close the Print Preview window and the Research task pane, if necessary.
10. Update and close the document.

Review questions

1. How do you open the Spelling and Grammar dialog box?

2 How does Word indicate a grammatical error?

　A With a wavy red underline

　B With a dot in the left margin

　C With a solid green underline

　D With a wavy green underline

3 Which automated feature is used to detect and fix errors or replace text as you type?

　A AutoCorrect

　B AutoText

　C AutoFormat

　D AutoSave

4 How do you turn off the automatic capitalization of the first letter of sentences?

5 What are the steps for finding specific text in a document?

6 How can you find only capitalized instances of a specific word in the document?

7 Select the best description of the Replace command.

　A It enables you to search for a specific word.

　B It enables you to check for misspelled words.

　C It enables you to search for specific text and replace it with different text.

　D It enables you to search for edited text and accept the changes.

8 When you use Quick Print, what is printed?

9 What should you do if you want to print only selected pages?

Unit 8
Graphics

Unit time: 30 minutes

Complete this unit, and you'll know how to:

A Insert graphics and clip art.

B Move graphics, wrap text around graphics, and modify graphics by cropping, rotating, and resizing them and by adjusting contrast in them.

Topic A: Adding graphics and clip art

This topic covers the following Microsoft Certified Application Specialist exam objective for Word 2007.

#	Objective
3.1.2	Insert pictures from files and clip art

Enhancing a document with graphics

Explanation

You can add graphics to Word documents by inserting your own graphics files, inserting clip art, or using Word's drawing tools to create your own graphic elements. After inserting graphics, you can modify them in a variety of ways, including resizing, cropping, and moving them.

To insert a graphic from a file:

1 In the document, place the insertion point where you want the graphic to appear.
2 Activate the Insert tab.
3 In the Illustrations group, click the Picture button to open the Insert Picture dialog box.
4 Navigate to the graphic you want to insert.
5 Select the graphic and click Insert.

When you insert or work with graphics or clip art, Word displays the Picture Tools. These are contained on a Format tab added to the Ribbon.

Graphics **8–3**

Do it! **A-1: Inserting a graphic**

Here's how	Here's why
1 Open Cookbook	From the current unit folder.
	This document is missing a graphic on one of the pages. You'll insert the missing graphic.
Save the document as **My cookbook**	In the current unit folder.
2 Move to page 14	(The Turmeric page.) Unlike the other pages in this section of the document, this one doesn't have a graphic.
3 Above "About this spice," place the insertion point as shown	**Turmeric**¶ Scientific·name:·Curcuma ¶ |¶ ¶ *About·this·spice*¶
4 Activate the Insert tab	
In the Illustrations group, click as shown	
	To open the Insert Picture dialog box.
5 Select the graphic **turmeric**	From the current unit folder.
Click **Insert**	To close the dialog box and insert the graphic. The Picture Tools appear, adding a Format tab to the Ribbon, with tools you can use to format the graphic.
6 Update and close the document	

Clip art

Explanation

Although you can insert your own graphics files into Word documents, you can also insert graphics from Word's extensive gallery of clip art. To insert clip art:

1 In the document, place the insertion point where you want the clip art to appear.
2 Activate the Insert tab.
3 In the Illustrations group, click Clip Art to display the Clip Art task pane.
4 Under Search for, enter a keyword describing the type of clip art you want to find, and then click Go. Word displays any clip art associated with the keyword. To view all available clip art, leave the Search for box blank and click Go.
5 Click the preview image of the clip art you want to use.

Graphics

Do it!

A-2: Inserting clip art

Here's how	Here's why
1 Open Graphics	From the current unit folder.
Save the file as **My graphics**	In the current unit folder.
2 Activate the Insert tab	To display the Insert options.
3 In the Illustrations group, click as shown	To display the Clip Art task pane.
4 In the Clip Art task pane, click **Go**	To display previews of the available clips in the Results box. A message box might appear, asking whether you want to search additional clips from online sources.
Click **No**	(If necessary.) It might take a moment for the clips to appear. You can use the vertical scrollbar to view them. You'll view only clips associated with food.
5 Under Search for, enter **Food**	
Click **Go**	Only clips associated with food appear.
6 Verify that the insertion point is at the beginning of the document	
7 Click the cornucopia image	The clip is inserted in the document, at the location of the insertion point.
8 Close the Clip Art task pane	
9 Update the document	

Topic B: Working with graphics

This topic covers the following Microsoft Certified Application Specialist exam objectives for Word 2007.

#	Objective
3.2.1	Format text wrapping
3.2.2	Format by sizing, cropping, scaling, and rotating
3.2.4	Set contrast, brightness, and coloration
3.2.6	Compress pictures

Options for working with graphics

Explanation

After you've inserted graphics, you can move them, change the way text wraps around them, and resize, rotate, and crop them. You can also change a graphic's contrast, brightness, and compression.

Moving a graphic

After you place a graphic, typically it will appear as an *inline graphic*, which moves along with the text as though it were a text character. When you click the graphic, selection handles appear around it, and the Picture Tools appear and are activated. (When Picture Tools are active, a Format tab is added to the Ribbon.) The Picture Tools groups are shown in Exhibit 8-1.

Exhibit 8-1: Picture tools

You can move an inline graphic by using any of the following methods:
- Cut the graphic and then paste it in the new location.
- Drag the graphic to the new location. (Avoid dragging the selection handles, or you will resize the graphic instead of moving it.)
- Select the graphic and activate the Picture Tools. On the Format tab, in the Arrange group, click Position and select an option from the list that appears.

When you select an option from the Position list, the graphic is positioned on the page as a *floating graphic*, and it no longer moves inline with the text. You can then drag the graphic to move it anywhere, and the text nearby will wrap around the graphic automatically.

Changing text-wrap options

You can change how text wraps, or flows, around a graphic. Using the Text Wrapping menu in the Arrange group, you can select the options shown in Exhibit 8-2.

Exhibit 8-2: The Text Wrapping menu

You can control a graphic's positioning and text wrapping with greater precision by using the Advanced Layout dialog box. For example, you can use this dialog box to specify values for the text-wrap distance.

To specify text-wrap distance values:

1. With the Picture Tools tab activated, click Text Wrapping and choose More Layout Options to open the Advanced Layout dialog box.
2. If necessary, activate the Text Wrapping tab, shown in Exhibit 8-3.
3. Under Distance from text, specify the minimum distance between text and each side of the graphic.
4. Click OK.

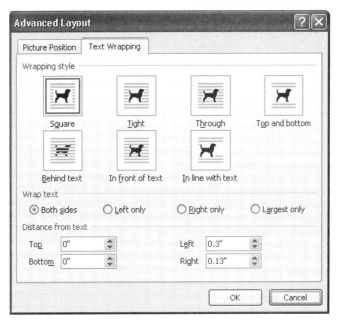

Exhibit 8-3: The Advanced Layout dialog box, showing the Text Wrapping options

Do it!

B-1: Controlling text flow around a graphic

Here's how	Here's why
1 Select the cornucopia clip	(If necessary.) White selection handles appear at each corner and along each side of the clip.
2 In the Arrange group, click **Position**	To display the Position gallery.
Point to several options in the gallery without clicking	To preview how each option will position the clip.
3 Under With Text Wrapping, point to the indicated option	
Click the top-right position option	To select it.
4 In the Arrange group, click **Text Wrapping**	To display the Text Wrapping menu, shown in Exhibit 8-2.
Verify that Square is selected	You'll move the text a bit farther from the graphic.
5 Choose **More Layout Options…**	(From the Text Wrapping menu.) To open the Advanced Layout dialog box.
Activate the Text Wrapping tab	
Under Distance from text, in the Left box, enter **0.3**	
Click **OK**	To close the dialog box. Now you'll drag the clip to adjust its position relative to the text.
6 Point to the cornucopia clip and drag slightly in any direction	To reposition it next to the paragraph. When you move the clip and release the mouse button, the text in the paragraph next to it re-flows.
7 Click in the document, away from the clip	To deselect the clip.
8 Update the document	

Resizing, rotating, and cropping graphics

Explanation

If you want to rotate, resize, or crop a graphic, it's often best to perform these types of transformations in the graphics application used to create the graphic. If that's not feasible, however, you can make some changes directly in Word.

Resizing graphics

When you resize a graphic, you should be cautious about increasing the size. In some cases, increasing a graphic's size too much can degrade its appearance significantly. However, you can typically decrease a graphic's size without degrading its appearance. After resizing graphics significantly, you might want to print a test copy of the document to ensure that you get the results you expect.

To resize a graphic:
1. Select the graphic you want to resize.
2. Point to a corner selection handle to resize the graphic proportionally, or point to a side selection handle to change just the graphic's width or height.
3. Drag the selection handle until the graphic is the size you want.

You can also resize a graphic by entering a specific percentage. To do so:
1. Right-click the graphic and choose Format Picture from the shortcut menu.
2. In the Format Picture dialog box, activate the Size tab.
3. Under Scale, in the Height and Width boxes, enter new percentages.
4. Click OK.

Rotating graphics

In addition to resizing a graphic, you might want to rotate it. As with resizing, you can rotate a graphic by dragging it or by entering a value in a dialog box.

To rotate a graphic manually:
1. Select the graphic.
2. Point to the green rotation handle at the top of the graphic. The pointer changes to a rotating arrow.
3. Drag to rotate the graphic.

To rotate a graphic numerically:
1. Right-click the graphic and choose Format Picture to open the Format Picture dialog box.
2. Activate the Size tab.
3. Under Rotate, in the Rotation box, enter the rotation value you want to use.
4. Click OK.

Cropping graphics

The process of removing a portion of a graphic is known as *cropping*. Unlike resizing, cropping changes the actual content of the graphic. Cropping can be used to remove extra white space around a graphic or to trim off a portion of a picture. Unless you specify otherwise (by checking "Delete cropped areas of pictures" in the Compression Settings dialog box), the entire picture is still available after you crop it.

To crop a graphic:

1. Select the graphic to be cropped.
2. In the Size group, click the Crop tool. The pointer changes to the crop symbol.
3. Point to an edge of the graphic and drag.

Graphics   8–11

Do it!   **B-2: Resizing and rotating a graphic**

Here's how	Here's why
1 Select the cornucopia clip	
2 Point to the top-right selection handle	 The pointer appears as a two-headed arrow.
3 Drag down and to the left, as shown	 To reduce the cornucopia's size by about one third.
4 Move the clip	To position it the way you want. Next, you'll rotate it.
5 Point to the green rotation handle at the top of the clip	 The pointer changes to a rotating arrow.
Drag to the right slightly	To rotate the clip slightly clockwise.
6 Adjust the clip's size, rotation, and position	To display the clip the way you want it.
7 Update the document	

Contrast, brightness, and compression

Explanation

In addition to changing the location and size of a graphic, you can change its color contrast and brightness. To do so, you can use the options in the Adjust group, shown in Exhibit 8-4.

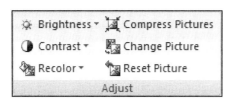

Exhibit 8-4: The Adjust group

To change a selected graphic's contrast and brightness, click Brightness or Contrast in the Adjust group and select a setting from the list. From either list, you can also choose Picture Corrections Options to open the Format Shape dialog box with the Picture option selected in the left pane. You can adjust the brightness and contrast by dragging sliders or by entering values. When you're finished, click Close to apply the settings you chose.

You can return the graphic to its original contrast and brightness by clicking Reset Picture.

Compressing a picture

You can apply compression to a picture to adjust its file size and quality. In the Adjust group, click Compress Pictures to open the Compress Pictures dialog box. Here, you can specify whether to apply settings to the selected graphic or to all graphics. In this dialog box, you can also click Options to open the Compression Settings dialog box.

In the Compression Settings dialog box, you can choose to delete cropped areas of a picture. You can also select the optimum quality of the image—the number of pixels per inch (ppi)—based on its purpose. For example, you can select the Print option (220 ppi) if you intend to print the document containing the image. This compression level is sufficient for paper output. However, if you want to send the document through e-mail, you'll want a smaller file size and can select the E-mail option (96 ppi).

Do it!

B-3: Adjusting contrast, brightness, and compression

Here's how	Here's why
1 Select the cornucopia clip	If necessary.
2 Activate the Picture Tools tab	If necessary.
3 In the Adjust group, click **Brightness**	To display the Brightness options.
Point to several values	To preview how each value will affect the graphic.
Select **-10%**	To darken the graphic slightly.
4 Click **Contrast** and select **+20%**	(In the Adjust group, on the Format tab.) To increase the contrast.
5 Click **Recolor**	(In the Adjust group.) To display the Recolor options.
Point to the option under No Recolor	(Don't click.) To preview how the graphic looked originally. You'll keep the modified settings.
Point away from the list and click	To close the list without selecting any options.
6 In the Adjust group, click **Compress Pictures**	To open the Compress Pictures dialog box.
Check **Apply to selected pictures only**	To apply compression settings to the selected picture.
Click **Options**	To open the Compression Settings dialog box.
7 Select **E-mail**	To select a compression level suitable for sending the document through e-mail.
Click **OK**	To close the Compression Settings dialog box.
Click **OK**	To close the Compress Pictures dialog box.
8 Update and close the document	

Unit summary: Graphics

Topic A   In this topic, you learned how to insert **graphics** and **clip art**.

Topic B   In this topic, you learned how to move graphics and how to modify graphics by **cropping**, **rotating**, and **resizing** them, adjusting their **contrast**, and **wrapping text** around them.

Independent practice activity

In this activity, you'll insert, position, and resize a clip art graphic. You'll also wrap text around the clip.

1. Open Update, and save it as **My update**.
2. Search for clip art associated with food, and insert the **apple for the teacher** clip at the beginning of the document. The clip is shown in Exhibit 8-5.
3. Position the clip in the document's top-right corner with tight text wrapping. (*Hint:* On the Picture Tools Format tab, in the Arrange group, click **Position** and select the appropriate setting.)
4. Adjust the size and position of the clip so it appears similar to Exhibit 8-6.
5. Update and close the file.
6. Close Word.

Exhibit 8-5: The "apple for the teacher" clip described in Step 2 of the independent practice activity

Exhibit 8-6: The clip as it appears in the document after Step 4 of the independent practice activity

Review questions

1 How can you move an inline graphic?

2 Describe the difference between an inline graphic and a floating graphic.

3 How can you open the Advanced Layout dialog box to specify text-wrap distance values?

4 How can you resize a selected graphic?

A Drag a selection handle.

B Select the Crop tool and drag a selection handle.

C Point to the green handle above the graphic and drag.

D Drag the Zoom slider in the window's bottom-right corner.

5 How can you adjust a selected graphic's contrast or brightness?

Course summary

This summary contains information to help you bring the course to a successful conclusion. Using this information, you will be able to:

A Use the summary text to reinforce what you've learned in class.

B Determine the next courses in this series (if any), as well as any other resources that might help you continue to learn about Word 2007.

Topic A: Course summary

Use the following summary text to reinforce what you've learned in class.

Unit summaries

Unit 1

In this unit, you learned that Word 2007 is a word processor. You started Word 2007 and explored its **environment**. Then you **created** and **saved** documents. You used the Save As command to save a document in a different folder and with a new file name, and you **renamed** a folder. Then you added text to a document and examined the nonprinting characters. Finally, you used the **Word Help** system.

Unit 2

In this unit, you **opened** a Word document, **navigated** with the scrollbars, and **moved** the insertion point with the keyboard. You also used the **Go To** command and the **Select Browse Object** button. You used Zoom options, and you learned about different **views**, including Print Layout view and Full Screen Reading view. Then you used the mouse, keyboard, and selection bar to **select text**.

Unit 3

In this unit, you **inserted** and **deleted** text and inserted the date and time in a document. In addition, you learned how to insert **symbols** and special characters. You also used the **Undo** and **Redo** commands. Finally, you **moved** and **copied** text and used the Paste Options button.

Unit 4

In this unit, you applied **character formatting**. Next, you used **tabs** to align text. Then you learned about basic **paragraph formatting**, such as changing paragraph alignment. You applied borders and shading, and added bulleted and numbered lists. You also set left and right **indents** and learned about hanging indents. Next, you set **paragraph spacing** and **line spacing**. Finally, you learned how to set AutoFormat options.

Unit 5

In this unit, you created a new **table** and converted text to a table. Then you **navigated** in a table and selected table elements. You added text to the table and applied character and paragraph formatting to it. Next, you modified tables by **adding rows** and **columns** and by deleting rows, columns, and tables. You also changed **column width**. Finally, you learned how to **align** tables.

Unit 6

In this unit, you inserted and edited **headers** and **footers**. You also inserted **page numbers** and set **margins** and page orientation. You also used **text-flow options**, such as widow/orphan control and "Keep with next." Finally, you inserted and deleted **page breaks**.

Unit 7

In this unit, you used the **Spelling and Grammar dialog box**. You also learned how to check spelling automatically. Then you used the grammar checker and the **thesaurus**. In addition, you added and used **AutoCorrect** entries. You also used the Find and Replace dialog box to locate and **replace** text. Finally, you used **Print Preview** and learned how to print a document by using the **Print** dialog box.

Unit 8

In this unit, you learned how to insert **graphics** and **clip art**. You also moved a graphic, learned how to resize, rotate, crop, and adjust contrast in graphics, and wrapped text around a graphic.

Topic B: Continued learning after class

It is impossible to learn to use any software effectively in a single day. To get the most out of this class, you should begin working with Word 2007 to perform real tasks as soon as possible. We also offer resources for continued learning.

Next courses in this series

This is the first course in this series. The next courses are:

- *Word 2007: Intermediate*
    - Create and modify styles
    - Create section breaks
    - Format and sort table data
    - Prepare and print labels and envelopes
    - Insert diagrams, text boxes, and shapes
    - Use templates and protect document contents
    - Track document revisions
    - Save a document as a Web page
- *Word 2007: Advanced*
    - Merge a recipient list with a form letter
    - Insert and modify objects
    - Use watermarks and themes
    - Create and protect forms
    - Use macros to automate tasks
    - Customize the Quick Access toolbar
    - Create a master document
    - Create an XML document
- *Word 2007: VBA Programming*
    - Build applications
    - Debug code
    - Automate data entry
    - Merge data files
    - Create forms
    - Build tables
    - Secure information
    - Share data

Other resources

For more information, visit www.axzopress.com.

Word 2007: Basic

Quick reference

Editing, formatting, and document management

Button	Shortcut keys	Function
		Displays a menu of commonly used file commands, such as Open, Save As, and Print.
¶		Shows or hides paragraph marks and other hidden formatting symbols (nonprinting characters).
		Shows or hides the rulers.
	CTRL + S	Saves the current document.
	CTRL + Z	Undoes the last action.
	CTRL + Y	Redoes the last action that was undone.
	CTRL + Y	Repeats the last action performed.
	CTRL + X	Cuts the selected text or object.
	CTRL + C	Copies the selected text or object.
	CTRL + V	Pastes the first text or object from the Clipboard.
		Copies the selected formatting and pastes it onto the next text you select.
B	CTRL + B	Applies bold formatting to the selected text.
I	CTRL + I	Applies italics to the selected text.
U	CTRL + U	Underlines the selected text.

Button	Shortcut keys	Function
≡	CTRL + L	Aligns the selected paragraph to the left.
≡	CTRL + E	Centers the selected paragraph.
≡	CTRL + R	Aligns the selected paragraph to the right.
≡	CTRL + J	Justifies the selected paragraph.
?	F1	Opens Word Help.
	CTRL + P	Opens the Print dialog box.
	F7	Opens the Spelling and Grammar dialog box.
	SHIFT + F7	Opens the thesaurus in the Research task pane.
	CTRL + F	Opens the Find and Replace dialog box.
	CTRL + ↵ ENTER	Inserts a manual page break at the insertion point.
	CTRL + DELETE	Deletes all the characters in a word after the insertion point.
	CTRL + ← BACKSPACE	Deletes all the characters in a word before the insertion point.

Navigation

Shortcut keys	Function
CTRL + ←	Moves the insertion point one word to the left.
CTRL + →	Moves the insertion point one word to the right.
CTRL + ↑	Moves the insertion point up one paragraph.
CTRL + ↓	Moves the insertion point down one paragraph.
CTRL + HOME	Moves the insertion point to the beginning of the document.
CTRL + END	Moves the insertion point to the end of the document.
SHIFT + TAB	In a table, moves one cell to the left.
ALT + HOME	In a table, moves to the first cell in a row.
ALT + END	In a table, moves to the last cell in a row.
ALT + PAGE UP	In a table, moves to the first cell in the column.
ALT + PAGE DOWN	In a table, moves to the last cell in the column

Selection techniques

Shortcut keys	Function
SHIFT + ←	Selects the text to the left of the insertion point one character at a time.
SHIFT + →	Selects the text to the right of the insertion point one character at a time.
SHIFT + ↑	Selects text from the left of the insertion point to the same position in the previous line.
SHIFT + ↓	Selects text from the right of the insertion point to the same position in the next line.
SHIFT + HOME	Selects text from the left of the insertion point to the beginning of the current line.
SHIFT + END	Selects text from the right of the insertion point to the end of the current line.

Glossary

Antonym
A word that has the opposite meaning of a given word.

Automatic page break
A page separator inserted by Word when text no longer fits on the current page.

Cell
In a table, the intersection of a row and a column.

Character format
Formatting that can be applied to any amount of text, from a single character to an entire document. Character formats include fonts, font styles, and font sizes.

Copy
A command that copies selected text or graphics to the Clipboard while leaving the selection in its original location in the document.

Cropping
The process of removing a portion of a graphic.

Cut
A command that removes selected text or graphics from the document and copies the selection to the Clipboard.

Document area
The part of a document that displays the text and graphics that you type and work with.

Floating graphic
A graphic that is placed independently of text, as opposed to an inline graphic.

Font
The design of a set of text characters.

Font styles
Boldface, italics, and underlining that can be applied to text. (Can also be called *type styles*.)

Footer
Text that prints at the bottom of a page, in the margin.

Hanging indent
A format in which all lines of a paragraph except the first are indented.

Header
Text that prints at the top of a page, in the margin.

Indent
The space between the left and right sides of a paragraph and the left and right margins of a page.

Inline graphic
A graphic that moves along with the text as though it were a text character, as opposed to a floating graphic.

Insertion point
A flashing vertical line that indicates where text will appear as you type in the document.

Leader
A series of characters (such as dots or dashes) that fill the space used by a tab character. Dot leaders are commonly used in tables of contents.

Line spacing
The amount of vertical space between the lines of a paragraph.

Manual page break
A separation you insert to start a new page.

Margins
The space between the document content and the top, bottom, left, and right edges of a page.

Nonprinting characters
Symbols that appear on the screen to represent actions on the keyboard, such as pressing Enter, Tab, or Spacebar.

Office button
A button that displays a menu of file-related commands, such as those for opening, saving, printing, and closing a document. Also provides access to the Word Options dialog box.

Office Clipboard
A temporary storage area that collects cut or copied content until you specify where to place it. The Office Clipboard can hold up to 24 items, which are displayed in the Clipboard task pane.

Orphan
A paragraph's first line printed by itself at the bottom of a page.

Page orientation
A setting that controls whether a page is set to print tall (portrait) or wide (landscape).

Pagination
The process of separating text into separate pages.

Paragraph spacing
The amount of vertical space between paragraphs.

Paste
A command used to insert text or other objects from the Clipboard.

Quick Access toolbar
A toolbar displaying buttons for frequently used commands (by default, Save, Undo, and Repeat/Redo). Can be customized.

Ribbon
A Word window component that contains tabs for Home, Insert, Page Layout, References, Mailings, Review, and View, as well as contextual tabs. Each tab contains several groups.

Ribbon groups
Collections of related tools and commands, displayed on the Ribbon. For example, tools and menus for changing font formats are arranged together in the Font group.

Sans serif font
A font that lacks the small lines of a serif font. The Arial font (used for the terms in this glossary) is an example.

Scrollbars
Shaded bars displayed along the right side and the bottom of the document window. Used to view parts of a document that don't currently fit in the window.

Selecting text
Highlighting text by using the mouse or the keyboard.

Selection bar
An area, located in the left margin of the document window, in which you click and drag to select lines, paragraphs, or an entire document.

Serif font
A type of font that has small lines at the top and bottom of letters. The Times New Roman font (used for these definitions) is an example.

Synonym
A word that has the same or similar meaning as another word.

Tab stops
Positions set on the horizontal ruler for the purpose of aligning text. Each time you press the Tab key, the text to the right of the insertion point is automatically moved to the next tab stop on the ruler.

Thesaurus
A resource that provides alternatives, or synonyms, for words.

White space
The blank areas of a document page.

Widow
A paragraph's last line, printed by itself at the beginning of a page.

Word-wrap
The feature that automatically moves the insertion point (and text) to the next line as you reach the end of the line of text you're typing.

Index

A

AutoCorrect
 Adding entries to, 7-16
 Described, 7-12
 Options for, 7-14
AutoFormat options, setting, 4-36
AutoRecover, 1-14

B

Borders, adding, 4-24
Bullets
 Adding to lists, 4-26
 Using pictures as, 4-27

C

Character formats
 Applying, 4-2, 4-6
 Removing, 4-4
 Repeating, 4-11
Clip art, 8-4
Clipboard, 3-10
Columns
 Adding to tables, 5-12
 Changing width of, 5-14
 Deleting, 5-14
Commands
 Redoing, 3-9
 Undoing, 3-8
Compression settings, 8-12
Copying and pasting, 3-14
Cutting and pasting, 3-10

D

Date-and-time field, inserting, 3-4
Default dictionary, changing, 7-3
Design tab
 For headers and footers, 6-2
 For tables, 5-2
Documents
 Browsing by object type, 2-12
 Creating, 1-7
 Going to a specific page in, 2-10
 Moving through, 2-7
 Opening, 2-2
 Previewing, 7-26
 Recovering, 1-14
 Saving, 1-11
 Saving in different formats, 1-13

F

File formats, 1-11
File location, changing, 1-14
Files, recently used, 2-2
Find command, 7-18
Floating graphics, 8-6
Folders
 Creating, 1-13
 Renaming, 1-17
Font styles, 4-3
Font, changing default, 4-6
Fonts, types of, 4-3
Footers
 Creating, 6-2
 Editing, 6-4
 For first page only, 6-4
 For odd and even pages, 6-4
Format Painter, 4-11
Format tab (Picture Tools), 8-2
Formatting
 Finding and replacing, 7-23
 Multiple selections, 7-23
Full Screen Reading view, 2-15

G

Galleries, 1-3
Go To command, 2-10
Grammar checking, 7-6
Graphics
 Changing brightness or contrast of, 8-12
 Cropping, 8-10
 Inserting, 8-2
 Moving, 8-6
 Resizing, 8-9
 Rotating, 8-9
 Wrapping text around, 8-7

H

Hanging indents, 4-30, 4-32
Headers
 Creating, 6-2
 Editing, 6-4
 For first page only, 6-4
 For odd and even pages, 6-4
Help system, 1-18
Hidden formatting symbols, 1-9
Hidden text, 4-6
Highlight tool, 4-9

I

Indent types and markers, 4-30
Inline graphics, 8-6

L

Layout tab (Table Tools), 5-2
Line breaks, adding, 4-32
Line spacing, 4-33, 4-34
Lists
    Adding bullets or numbering to, 4-26
    Modifying, 4-27
Live Preview, 1-3

M

Magnifying documents, 2-5
Margins, setting, 6-7, 6-9
Mini toolbar, 4-2

N

Nonprinting characters, 1-9

O

Office button, 1-3
Office Clipboard, 3-10

P

Page breaks, inserting and deleting, 6-14
Page numbering, adding, 6-6
Page orientation, 6-10
Paragraph formats
    Alignment, 4-23
    Indents, 4-30
    Line spacing, 4-33, 4-34
    Repeating, 4-22
    Space before and after, 4-33
    Text-flow options, 6-12
Paste Options button, 3-11
Paste Special command, 4-12
Picture files, compressing, 8-12
Picture Tools, 8-6
Print Layout view, 2-13
Print options, 7-28
Print Preview, 7-26

Q

Quick Access toolbar, 1-3

R

Redo command, 3-9
Repeat command, 4-11, 4-22
Replace command, 7-21
Research task pane, 7-9
Ribbon, 1-3

Header & Footer Tools, 6-2
Picture Tools, 8-2
Table Tools, 5-2
Rows
    Adding to tables, 5-12
    Deleting, 5-14

S

Save command, 1-11
Scrolling techniques, 2-5
Select Browse Object button, 2-12
Selection bar, 2-22
Serif vs. sans serif fonts, 4-3
Shading, adding, 4-24
Special characters, inserting, 3-6
Spelling
    Checking, 7-2
    Checking as you type, 7-5
Splitting a window, 2-8
Symbols, inserting, 3-6

T

Tables
    Adding rows and columns to, 5-12
    Adding text to, 5-10
    Aligning, 5-16
    Changing column width in, 5-14
    Converting to text, 5-18
    Creating, 5-2
    Deleting rows and columns in, 5-14
    Formatting text in, 5-11
    Moving in, 5-7
    Selecting elements in, 5-8
Tabs
    Applying a leader, 4-20
    Clearing, 4-18
    Dialog box, 4-19
    Moving, 4-16
    Setting, 4-16
    Types of, 4-14
Task panes
    Clip Art, 8-4
    Clipboard, 3-10
    Research, 7-9
Templates, 1-8
Text
    Aligning vertically, 6-10
    Converting to a table, 5-5
    Copying, 3-14
    Cutting and pasting, 3-10
    Deleting, 3-2
    Entering, 1-9
    Finding, 7-18
    Hiding, 4-6
    Highlighting, 4-9
    Replacing, 7-21
    Selecting by dragging, 2-17
    Selecting with the keyboard, 2-20

Selecting with the selection bar, 2-22
Sorting, 4-28
Text-wrap options, 8-7
Thesaurus, 7-8

U

Undo command, 3-8

V

Views
Full Screen Reading, 2-15
Print Layout, 2-13

W

Widow/orphan control, 6-12
Window, splitting, 2-8
Word
Compatibility with previous versions, 1-11
Window components, 1-2

X

XML file format, 1-12

Z

Zoom slider, 2-5